Patnude

A Storied Life

WRITTEN BY

Jack Larsen

INKWELL BOOKS

Writing · Publishing · Printing

ISBN: 978-0-9852501-8-8
Library of Congress Control Number: 2019904692

Published by Inkwell Books LLC
10632 North Scottsdale Road, Unit 695
Scottsdale, AZ 85254
Tel. 480-315-3781
E-mail info@inkwellbooksllc.com
Website www.inkwellbooksllc.com

INKWELL BOOKS
Writing · Publishing · Printing

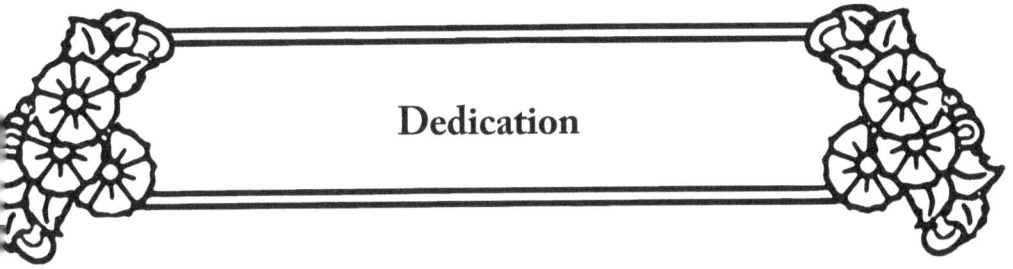

Dedication

"Patnude" is dedicated to my favorite and very special cousin Val Marie (Dolly) Wilson, who is no longer with us. I frequently thought of Dolly as I was writing "Patnude." I know she would have enjoyed reading it, at least that is what Dolly would have told me.

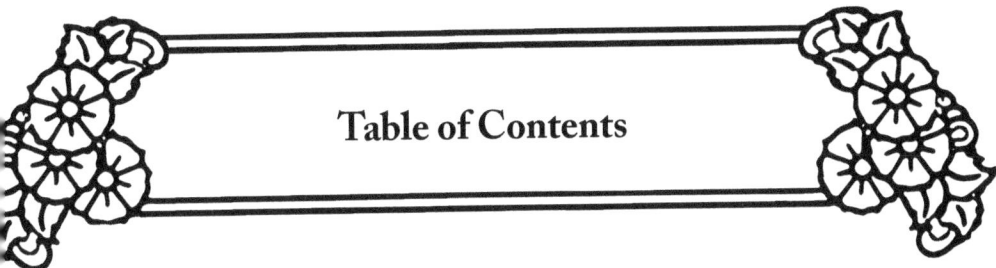

Table of Contents

Patnude Finds Happiness
on Arizona Route 77

Patnude Sheekey picked up Stuart Scott Shurts in Green Valley and was bringing him to his funeral at Forever Restful Cemetery in Globe at 2:00 p.m. this afternoon. Patnude worked for Best Funeral Home, also in Globe, and more specifically for Mr. I.M. Best.

Stuart Scott Shurts was resting in the coffin that was in the back of the small rented 4-cylinder Hyundai SUV that Patnude was driving. He wished he had rented a Chevy Suburban with a big V8, as Route 77 is a twisty two-lane highway over the mountains. So far, Patnude was right on schedule. He should have Stuart Scott Shurts at his gravesite in time for his service and burial. He knew I.M. would go nuts if he was late with Stuart.

Starting to climb one of the mountains, Patnude got behind a loaded semi-truck and trailer that was going about 25 mph. It was okay, as he just passed a "Passing Lane" sign stating the passing lane was 3 miles ahead. He did the calculation in his head on how long it would take him to go 3 miles at 25 mph. Patnude was patient. He looked in his rear view mirror and saw a Corvette with a small line of cars behind it.

He passed the 2 mile sign, then the 1 mile sign, then the 1,000 feet sign, then the 500 feet sign. He was ready to cut into the passing lane when he saw the Arizona highway sign, "Passing Lane Closed for Repairs." *Oh no*, he thought. However, he remembered there is another passing lane about 5 miles or so just ahead. A mile or so up Arizona Route 77 he saw the passing lane sign stating the distance to the next passing lane. He was now doing 30 mph. He did the math again. Patnude now knew there were three semi-trucks and trailers in front of him.

The line behind him was getting longer, and the Corvette was right on his ass. He was nervous. He passed all of the passing lane signs again: 4 miles, 3 miles, 2 miles, 1 mile, 1,000 feet and 500 feet.

Patnude knew he would have to lurch out into the passing lane to avoid being stuck behind the three trucks. He was cursing again to himself on why he got stuck with the underpowered 4-cylinder Hyundai.

The passing lane was open. He darted into the left lane before the Corvette. He was now up to 40 mph as he passed the first truck, then 50 mph as he passed the second truck, with the Corvette still on his ass. At almost 55 mph, he passed the third and last truck. He quickly cut into the right lane ahead of the last truck.

The Corvette blew its horn and the driver gave Patnude the finger as he and the long line of cars passed him. He didn't care as he looked at his watch and confirmed to himself that he and Stuart would just make it in time for Stuart's graveside service and subsequent burial.

Patnude then realized that he had just found happiness in the passing lane on Arizona Route 77 somewhere between Tucson and Globe.

PASSING LANE 100 MILES AHEAD

In The Distance

Patnude continued driving the small Hyundai SUV with Stuart Scott Shurts in the back resting in his coffin on their drive to Globe.

Patnude pulled into Forever Restful Cemetery at 1:52 p.m. and parked at Stuart Scott Shurt's gravesite at 1:55 p.m., just in time for the 2:00 p.m. service. His boss, I.M. Best, looked at his watch and breathed a sigh of relief. Several of the cemetery workers quickly and silently removed the coffin from the Hyundai SUV and carried it to Stuart Scott Shurt's gravesite. Patnude counted only four people at the gravesite, the minister, a man and two women, and of course the cemetery workers.

Patnude observed that Stuart had a large upright headstone in place. At the top of the headstone in large block letters was "Stuart Scott Shurts" and under it in even larger block letters was "In The Distance."

Patnude wondered what "In The Distance" meant, especially on a headstone. He thought he remembered a song by Bette Midler with "distance" in the title, but he wasn't quite sure. His curiosity got the best of him and he stopped the man after the burial service to inquire.

"Excuse me, sir. I'm Patnude Sheekey with Best Funeral home and I was wondering what 'In The Distance' on the headstone means?"

"Patnude, I'm Scott Stuart Shurts and these are my sisters, Susan Sally Shurts and Sally Susan Shurts."

Patnude had a sort of blank look on his face.

Scott recognized the blank look from previous family introductions. "Our parents only knew or liked two male and two female children names that began with S. Therefore, they were restricted to a maximum of four children. Hence, my deceased brother was Stuart Scott, I'm Scott Stuart and my two sisters are Susan Sally and Sally Susan. Actually, it's quite simple."

Patnude nodded like he understood.

"Now to answer your question regarding 'In The Distance,' I believe each one of us will have a different answer. Susan, why don't you go first?"

"Well, Patnude, 'in the distance' was a phrase Stuart used most of his life. He would use it when he answered questions or made statements. His houseboat on Lake Powell was named 'In The Distance' and his speed boat 'In The Distance II.' When he had an airplane, it was named 'In The Distance.' Oh, and years ago he owned a local travel agency and it was called 'In The Distance Travel.' We decided 'In The Distance' was a perfect inscription on Stuart's headstone."

Patnude listened and nodded his understanding.

Scott began, "I will have a little different answer than Susan. Although all of her comments are correct. Stuart learned the phrase from a crossword puzzle he was doing when he was a teenager. I think he was 14 or 15 at the time. It somehow seemed like magic to him. He started using the phrase 'in the distance' from then on. He would get excited when he found it again in another crossword puzzle he was doing. I remember he called me when he first heard Paul Simon's song, 'Train In The Distance.' That song and Bette Midler's song, 'From A Distance' became his favorite songs. Oh, he also called me when he read Jack Dylan's poem 'In The Distance,' which then became his favorite poem."

Susan interrupted, "What about the Blutengel's song, 'In The Distance'?" He heard it not long after it was distributed. He called all of us on it. I think the group is from Germany, but I'm not sure."

"Sally you're next," Scott said.

"Again, all of the above comments are true and actually occurred. However, I have a little different interpretation on why Stuart used it."

"I believe it gave Stuart wiggle room to avoid answering a question. It gave him an easy out and left the questioner wondering and trying to interpret the meaning of Stuart's answer. He used to create the illusion he could see into the future—which he couldn't, I might add. He also used it to try and convince the listener that he had a vision to see far away, different than looking into the future. Also, reaching for something in the distance. Finally, my brother liked to, and did, procrastinate and 'in the distance' was the perfect response to get Stuart off the hook from performing. As you can tell, I'm the pragmatic one of the family."

Scott and Susan said in unison, "Sally is the pragmatic one."

"I hope this answers your question on what 'In The Distance' means on Stuart's headstone," Scott said.

Patnude was quiet, thinking for about 10 seconds. "Yes, it does. Thank you for sharing your thoughts with me."

As Scott, Susan and Sally walked away from Stuart's gravesite, Patnude determined "In The Distance" was Scott, Susan and Sally's way of remembering, with love in their hearts, their brother Stuart.

Patnude Meets Scoop Cooper

Patnude watched the cemetery workers as they started to backfill the gravesite of Stuart Scott Shurts. He once again stared at the inscription on the headstone: "In The Distance."

He walked slowly to the Best Funeral Home's rented SUV and made the decision that he was not going to drive it on Arizona Route 77 with a body in back ever again. As Patnude opened the driver's door, a beat-up white Ford LTD 4-door which appeared to be an old police cruiser, pulled up fast and slid to a stop on the gravel cemetery driveway across from Patnude's parked Hyundai.

The driver had the door open before the old Ford stopped. He jumped out exactly when it stopped. He was short, overweight, and balding with a comb-over. His glasses were large and thick with black plastic frames. He was wearing a bright green short-sleeved shirt with large yellow flowers on it, dark brown cargo shorts with bulging pockets, and sandals with calf-length black socks that had several holes in them. He had an owl-like expression. He stopped and looked at Patnude.

"Hi, I'm Clyde 'Scoop' Cooper with the Arizona News. You can call me Scoop. Here's my card.

"Is this where Stuart Scott Shurts' funeral is going to be?"

"Hello, I'm Patnude Sheekey. Mr. Shurts' funeral is over and everyone has left."

"Nuts. I got lost and couldn't find the cemetery. I was afraid I was going to be late. I was supposed to interview Shurts' relatives. They've left, haven't they?"

"Yes, they left the cemetery about a half hour ago."

"Do you know where they were going?"

"No, I don't. Why do you want to interview them?"

"You don't know anything about 'In The Distance Shurts' do you?"

"No, I don't."

"Well," Scoop exclaimed, "let me tell you about Stuart Scott Shurts' alias—'In The Distance Shurts'."

Patnude Meets Boo Boo

Patnude spent the next 15 or 20 minutes listening to Scoop explain about Stuart Scott Shurts' alias.

Patnude couldn't tell if he was impressed, overwhelmed or bored. He listened while he watched Scoop and he slowly nodded his head from time to time.

"It's late, and I have another story to follow up with," Scoop stated. He jumped in the old Ford LTD, started it up, yanked the wheel to the left, gave it gas spinning the tires on the loose gravel, made a U-turn running off the road onto the grass and departed Forever Restful Cemetery passing a silver Rolls Royce entering the cemetery.

Patnude watched the silver Rolls Royce pull up and stop in front of him. The driver lowered the window.

"Are you Patnude Sheekey? Mr. Best said you would still be here. We would like to talk with you. Do you have a minute?"

Patnude nodded, and said, "Yes, I do." The rear windows of the silver Rolls Royce were dark tinted so Patnude could not view the passenger.

The driver opened the door, but he didn't get out quickly, nor did he get out slowly—he got out with a potent attitude.

Patnude decided he was more, much more than a chauffeur. The trunk opened automatically and the man removed a pair of small walking shoes, most likely for a woman. The rear door opened and the man handed the shoes to a woman.

The woman swung her legs out, removed her black pumps and put on the black walking shoes. Her black nylons highlighted her legs. Patnude couldn't help notice the large diamond rings, one on each of her hands. A large diamond bracelet was on her right wrist, and a gold Rolex watch with a diamond face she wore on her left wrist.

Patnude concluded he knew who owned the silver Rolls Royce.

She almost sprang out of the car. Her black skirt was cut to the middle of her

Betty Grable legs. Under her black blazer she wore a bright orange turtleneck sweater, which highlighted a diamond cluster necklace. Her hair was silver, cut into a bob which framed her controlling face. Her large gold framed sunglasses covered her eyes.

Patnude reached the logical conclusion he was about to meet an attractive, mature and powerful woman.

She walked briskly towards Patnude with a warm smile, which highlighted her perfect white teeth and her right hand reached out to shake hands with Patnude.

The man followed off to her right side with a protective posture.

Her handshake was warm, firm, controlling and long lasting.

"Mr. Sheekey, I'm Bailee Braylee Shurts and this is Augie Control. However, you can just call me Boo Boo. I am Stuart's aunt and I raised him from almost a baby. I just have a few questions about Stuart's funeral, and then I wanted to pay my respects at his gravesite."

"Pleased to meet you, Boo Boo and Augie. Please, call me Patnude."

Patnude's Analysis of
Mr. Lee Roy Stroskey

Best Funeral Home specialized in providing a personal care service to the surviving family who lived in the Globe-Miami area.

I.M. Best sent Patnude to the home of the widow of Lee Roy Stroskey, who died two days ago, to select the last suit Mr. Stroskey would wear.

Patnude examined the ten suits hanging in Mr. Stroskey's closet. He selected a dark blue suit, a white shirt and a red tie.

"That was Lee Roy's favorite suit, shirt and tie," Mrs. Stroskey said. "I can still hear him saying he felt and looked presidential when he wore it."

As usual, when Patnude returned to Best Funeral Home he would examine the pockets of the deceased's final and permanent outfit. He would then try and analyze what the items he found would tell him about the deceased person. He usually left the items in the pockets where he found them, but would prepare a list for the deceased's loved ones.

This is what he found in the pockets of Mr. Lee Roy Stroskey's favorite dark blue suit:

* Business card from The Italian Restaurant with a red finger smudge on it
* A quarter dated 1940
* Half of a Kleenex Pocket-Pack
* A Splenda packet
* A dark blue plastic ball point pen
* A slip of folded paper with 6 phone numbers, with initials in front of each phone number
* An aspirin tin with 2 tablets inside
* Eight one-dollar bills paper clipped together

Patnude studied the above items for five or ten minutes before he concluded his analysis of Mr. Lee Roy Stroskey, which is as follows:

* Mr. Stroskey had good taste in clothes, dressed conservatively and was conscious of his appearance.

* He liked to eat. His favorite food was Italian and his favorite restaurant was The Italian Restaurant.

* He was somewhat superstitious as he carried the 1940 quarter for good luck, since his date of birth was January 1, 1940.

* The half pocket-pack of Kleenex indicated Mr. Stroskey suffered from allergies and/or sinus issues.

* The Splenda packet suggested Mr. Stroskey was watching his calories and avoiding sugar; however, his fondness for Italian food most likely overruled his self-control.

* Mr. Stroskey liked to be prepared and be able to record any new thing of importance that occurred in his life. Therefore he carried a dark blue plastic ball point pen.

* The slip of paper recorded the key phone numbers he might need. Again, another indication of being an organized and prepared person.

* He must have had some pain issues that arose from time to time; therefore he carried the aspirin tin. With only two left, it was apparent the issues were current. Nonetheless, he was prepared.

* Finally, the eight dollar bills support a man wanting to be prepared for the unexpected, however, conservative as he did not want to carry excessive cash.

In summary, Patnude concluded that Mr. Lee Roy Stroskey was a well-dressed man who planned to always be prepared, had some sinus/allergy issues, suffered some pain from time to time, loved Italian food, but was calorie conscious and was a little superstitious.

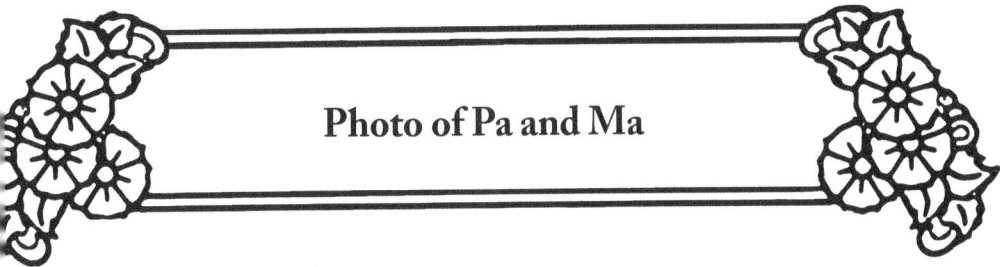

Photo of Pa and Ma

Patnude looked tired, and was tired, as he dragged himself into his apartment. It took him longer than anticipated to prepare Lee Roy Stroskey for his final viewing at Best Funeral Home.

The darkness of his apartment always depressed Patnude, and the first thing he always did was to turn all the lights on. The last room he lit up, as usual, was his bedroom. Patnude's scowl or frown turned into a slight smile when his bedroom glowed from the ceiling light. He'd once again looked at the large framed photo of his grandparents, placed on the right side of his dresser. He would look at the photo at least twice a day. His grandparents raised him since he was five. He called them Pa and Ma. They are both gone now.

The black and white photo was taken in 1939 and Pa and Ma were on their honeymoon in Northern Arizona. It was a rustic setting with trees and a low flat rock fence in the background. It was a staged photo as Ma was a big woman and stood at least a foot taller than Pa, but Pa was standing on a large rock alongside Ma, and now he was the tall one. His left arm was behind her, and her arms were wrapped behind her back. Patnude knew they were holding hands. Their smiles were genuine. Pa was dressed in his favorite outfit, white shirt, dark pants and highly polished shoes. Pa had always been fussy about the shine on his shoes.

Patnude looked down at his own shoes and saw that they were also highly polished, even at the end of a workday.

Ma was wearing a print dress with a belt; the hem, of course, fell below her knees. Her shoes were white, with no heels. Their dark hair would eventually turn to gray.

They both looked overdressed for the rural setting, but that was always Pa and Ma's style.

Patnude smiled again as he remembered Ma always saying that she thought Pa hadn't finished growing when she married him. Pa replied, after he married Ma, nobody picked on the short man anymore.

I.M.'s Art Gallery Room

Patnude was sitting on the large brown leather chair facing I.M.'s desk. He was looking at the framed black and white photo of I.M., placed on the right side of his desk facing the chair for the visitor to view while meeting with I.M.

I.M., in his own way, considered himself an art collector. The black and white photograph of himself along with four other art works, were staged in his art gallery room on the second floor of his house.

In the photograph I.M. was leaning against a closed door with his right shoulder, the lights dimmed. He was dressed in his proper funeral parlor clothes, white long-sleeved shirt, light colored tie with small dark symmetrical squares and dark trousers. His hair was poofed-up for the photograph and he had a somber artistic expression on his face as he looked down at the plaster cast of a woman's face that was resting on his left shoulder. Attached to the door and above I.M.'s left shoulder was a plaster cast of a large man's right hand. Off to I.M.'s right side hanging on the wall, almost life size, was an intricate wire sculpture of a man and woman facing each other. Hanging under the wire sculpture was a framed pen and ink drawing of a woman sitting on a chair. Underneath the pen and ink drawing was a large piece of woven cloth with intricate designs fastened to the wall.

The framed black and white photograph had an artistic touch to it, which was I.M.'s goal.

John W. Snow's
Good Luck Stone

The viewing of the deceased, John W. Snow, began on Thursday at 11:00 a.m. at Best Funeral Home in Globe, Arizona.

John W. Snow was known as Johnny to everyone who knew him. He died on his 32nd birthday.

As usual, Patnude was standing near the open coffin.

At 11:30 a.m., a tall woman wearing jeans, a blue blazer, a man's light blue long-sleeved shirt with a button-down collar and dark brown penny loafers with a penny in each loafer strap approached John W. Snow's coffin. Her eyes were bright blue and her long auburn hair was straight and reached the middle of her back. Her bright red lipstick highlighted her face, which displayed a somber expression.

Patnude observed a sad, attractive woman.

She leaned over and whispered in John W. Snow's ear at the same time she placed a small, highly polished multi-colored grey stone on his chest. The grey stone was oblong and about the size of a large eraser. The multi-colored tones of the grey stone were separated by irregular whitish grey lines. Before she finished whispering in John W. Snow's ear, she picked up the stone from his chest with her left hand and slid it into John W. Snow's stiff right hand. When she straightened up she noticed Patnude watching her. She smiled as she took a few steps towards Patnude.

"That was Johnny's good luck stone. He always carried it in his right front pants pocket since he was a teenager. It always brought him good luck. I'm Johnny's sister, Jackie Snow."

"Pleased to meet you Jackie. I'm Patnude Sheekey with Best Funeral Home. "

"I know what you are thinking," Jackie said, looking straight into Patnude's eyes. "If that is Johnny's good luck stone, what is he doing lying in the coffin?" as she touched Johnny's chest with her right hand.

Patnude nodded his head, yes.

"Well my dumb-ass brother left his good luck stone laying on the kitchen countertop when he went for his last motorcycle ride."

Patnude Visits The Complete Hardware & Variety Store in Miami, Arizona

Patnude had the afternoon off and drove down to Miami. He parked his car on the north end of town and walked down Sullivan Street. He stopped in front of an old abandoned two-story building and stared at it. He always felt sad when he looked at the building. The sign above the store's front windows was faded with peeling paint. However, he could still read the name, The Complete Hardware & Variety Store. Underneath, in small print, was "Everything You Need."

It was his grandparent's hardware and variety store. He was raised on the second floor above the store. His grandfather ran the hardware section and his grandmother the variety section. Pa and Ma are both gone now.

He walked across the street to look into the store's windows. The glass was dirty and he had to wipe a spot clean with his handkerchief so he could see into the old store. He saw empty counters and shelves. The store was dirty and covered with heavy dust. Empty cardboard boxes were scattered around. Many of the ceiling tiles had fallen on top of the counters. On the left side against the wall of the abandoned Hardware & Variety Store he saw something that made him smile. Nail bins. He counted them, as he had many times in the past, and there still were 12 nail bins. The customers, when selecting the nails they needed, always mixed up the nails from one bin to another. Patnude's grandfather used to pay him $1.00 every week to properly organize the nail bins. Patnude remembered he used to argue with Pa that he should receive $.10 per bin and since there were 12 bins, his compensation should be $1.20. Pa replied he would only pay $.083 per bin. That's all he could afford. Every week Patnude always organized 12 nail bins and Pa only and always paid him $1.00.

Upon further reflection, Patnude had a stark realization. He wondered if Ma mixed up the nails so he had a way to earn a $1.00.

Oh well, it doesn't matter now he thought, *since nails only come in boxes now.*

Patnude turned around and walked back up Sullivan Street to his car.

THE COMPLETE HARDWARE & VARIETY STORE

Home Is

"Home is Best and Best Is Your Final Home" is Best Funeral Home's slogan. It's stated on the letterhead, business cards, funeral and burial contracts, and on the sign above the door to the entrance of Best Funeral Home in Globe, Arizona.

Every July 4th, the town of Globe celebrates by holding its "Old Fashioned Independence Day Celebration." I.M. requires Patnude to man Best Funeral Home's table that is set up on Broad Street.

The table has a stack of brochures for the funeral home and Best Funeral Home's annual contest for the best description of "Home is ???." I.M. picks the winner, who will receive $65.00 cash and a $500.00 gift certificate to be used whenever at Best Funeral Home.

Of course, Best Funeral Home's slogan hangs from the table. Using its slogan "Home Is Best and Best Is Your Final Home" disqualifies you from the contest.

For the most part, Patnude enjoys working the table every July 4th. But from time to time, some of the patrons from local bars harass him.

This year's worst harassment was when two rather large redneck pickup truck cowboys pulled their pants down exposing their large, fat butts and bent over in front of Patnude and shouted, "Home is you kissing my ass."

The redneck pickup truck cowboys laughed as they pulled up their pants and stumbled down Broad Street to the next open bar.

Some of this year's July 4th contest entries are as follows:

Home is where the heart is.

Home is whenever I'm with you.

Home is the hunter.

Home is where I don't want to be.

Home is perfect.

Home is an old trailer.

Home is where love begins.

Home is possible.

Home is where you make it.

Home is where families are found.

Home is my past.

Home is where all my money goes.

Home is where all my memories are.

Home is my future.

Home is best.

Home is where the dog is.

Home is where my story begins.

Home is where I can't wait to leave.

Home is where they sent me when I was released.

I.M. carefully reviewed all of the entries. As usual there were almost 25 entries with "Home is where the heart is." Patnude knew they would never win.

I.M. selected "Home is best" as the winner of the annual 4th of July contest. The winner was Famine Kumar, from Miami, Arizona. She looked familiar to Patnude.

Famine was a rather large woman with bright red, silver and blue hair, wearing an American flag dress. The stars and stripes were stretched pretty thin across her mid-section. She was wearing large sunglasses with red, white and blue frames. Her upper lip had bright blue lipstick and her lower lip bright red lipstick, so when she smiled you saw red, white and blue, which matched her tennis shoes that were painted red, white and blue. Famine was "Miss 4th of July."

Patnude photographed Famine hugging I.M. and buoyantly waving her $65 dollars in cash and her $500.00 gift certificate from Best Funeral Home in front of I.M.'s face.

Patnude saw I.M. smiling and thought I.M. was enjoying the long powerful hug from Famine.

At the end of the 4th of July parade, Patnude began cleaning up Best Funeral Home's display and carrying the table, chairs, brochures and whatever to his car.

He looked up Broad Street and noticed the rather large woman with red, silver and blue hair wearing the tightly stretched American flag dress walking with I.M. It struck him when he'd seen her before, a slightly younger and slimmer winner of the Best Funeral Home's 4th of July contest in prior years.

Liver and Onions

This was a busy week for Patnude at Best Funeral Home. It was Wednesday, and they'd already had four services. Three of them included burials. He worked late tonight to get the deceased ready for tomorrow's viewing and subsequent burial. Patnude was sad, as the deceased was a 30-year-old woman from Miami who had committed suicide with a 22-caliber pistol. Her name was Carissa Shukla. Patnude went to high school with her. Everybody called her Cari. Patnude and Cari dated for a while in high school and remained friends over the years.

Patnude wondered how Cari would feel lying naked in front of him now. He certainly tried back in high school to get Cari's clothes off. He remembered how excited he was, and he thought Cari was also, when he slipped his hand under her bra and caressed her large, firm breasts. He was sure Cari would be embarrassed if she knew she was lying naked on a table in front of him now.

Cari had long brown hair and Patnude was able to conceal the wound from the gunshot to her head. She was attractive and almost looked like she was merely sleeping as she laid there after Patnude dressed her in her dark blue dress highlighted by her white pearl necklace. Patnude was tired and depressed when he left Best Funeral Home. He decided to dine out tonight since it was 7:30 and he did not feel like cooking.

His favorite restaurant was the Le Citron Restaurant in Globe. The hostess, Mary Ellen, recognized him and gave him a quiet table by the fireplace. He ordered a glass of Merlot. He perused the menu and saw the special for the evening was liver and onions with a side of spinach. It had been years since he had liver and onions. It was one of Pa's favorite meals, and he remembered that Ma made some kind of liver and onions once a week.

Patnude ordered the special with a side of spinach, and smiled to himself, thinking of his Ma and Pa. Just as he forked a slab of liver into his mouth, he noticed it was smothered in catsup. He then remembered how he disliked liver and onions, but his Ma and Pa made him eat it until he left Miami for the U of A. He hadn't had liver and onions since he left the hardware store in Miami. He ordered another glass of Merlot, finished the side of spinach and pushed the catsup-coated liver and onions off to the side. He remembered no matter how Ma cooked the liver and onions, he disliked it. In fact, he hated liver and onions.

Thursday night, Patnude and I.M. just finished preparing the deceased, Herbert Liter, for his viewing, service and burial for the following day.

"Patnude, I know this has been a busy, difficult week. Would you like to come over late Saturday afternoon for dinner and drinks? Famine will join us, and you can bring someone."

Patnude accepted, since I.M. always put on a spread with great food and liquor. It was just what he needed. He thought he might ask Jackie Snow to join him, as they had gone out for coffee several times since meeting her at her brother's funeral.

It was 4:00 p.m. on Saturday when Patnude and Jackie pulled onto I.M.'s circular driveway. I.M. and Famine greeted them and quickly ushered them in and mixed them a drink.

Patnude observed that Famine was attractive for a large woman. She no longer had her 4th of July hair of red, silver and blue. It was now blonde. Famine wore a long black sleeveless dress and a large gold chain necklace with a magnifying glass attached. Patnude thought for a second he missed her 4th of July outfit. Famine still used her bright red lipstick, but this time it was on both her upper and lower lips.

I.M. announced that, "Famine was making dinner tonight. It's her specialty and a favorite that everybody loves."

"What is it?" Patnude asked.

"Liver and onions with a side of spinach," I.M. answered.

Patnude downed all of his Manhattan.

The Funeral of Sweenie Muldoon

The funeral service for Mrs. Sweenie Muldoon was scheduled to start at 11:00 a.m. on Thursday. Sissie Muldoon, her granddaughter, was to give the eulogy.

Patnude counted 9 people at the service: Sissie and her 3 boyfriends, Rob, Robbie and Robert; Grandma Sweenie's four neighbors, Maddie, Greta, Louise and Anna; and Seth Ostler, an old friend of Grandma Sweenie's from high school and her old boss at Mountain States Telephone and Telegraph Company.

Seth was wearing a dark brown suit jacket, which he kept buttoned, and a white shirt with a red tie. He waddled when he walked, which brought attention to the slightly too big overalls he wore underneath his suit jacket. He preferred standing over sitting.

Sissie began very solemnly, and her eyes were tearing.

"It is with great sadness that we are all gathered here today for the funeral of my grandmother, Sweenie Muldoon. Her heart attack was totally unexpected, and her death was a shock to all of us. Grandma Sweenie will be missed by all of us who knew and loved her."

Sissie's eyes continued to tear, as were Seth's when he finally sat down.

"I'm sad to say that Grandpa Boris had a prior commitment and has been detained. He is unable be here today."

"Grandma was always a special person to me. I always wanted to be like her. She showed me how to love and enjoy life. She liked the outdoors, exercise, being with close friends and feeling close to nature. I remember many good times sitting at her picnic table in her backyard having a glass of milk and chocolate chip cookies from Bashas'. Everybody who knew Grandma knew she couldn't cook or bake anything. When I was a teenager, we frequently sat at her picnic table having wine and cheese and crackers, and eventually just wine. Her picnic table will always be special to me and bring fond memories of Grandma. She loved sitting in her backyard at her picnic table. It was her favorite place to be in the whole world."

Sissie looked at her grandmother, lying in her coffin. She kissed her on the forehead, looked at the 8 people in attendance and said, "Grandma, you will always be in our hearts and you will be missed by all of us. Thank you all for attending today; we will leave in a few minutes for Grandma's burial at Forever Restful Cemetery."

As Seth Ostler stood up, tears were running down his cheeks.

Patnude drove the hearse. I.M. sat in the passenger seat, and Grandma Sweenie laid in her coffin.

I.M. looked over at Patnude and said, "That went better than I expected. Not bad at all."

Patnude nodded as he slowly drove to the Forever Restful Cemetery. Four cars followed the hearse.

"What really happened?" Patnude asked.

I.M. smiled before he answered.

"Well, Grandma Sweenie did die from a heart attack. That was true. However, it happened when she was running naked from her backyard with Seth Ostler, who was also naked, as they were being chased by Grandpa Boris, who had a shotgun. It seems Grandma Sweenie and Seth were having intercourse on top of her favorite picnic table in her backyard. Which I understand they did on a somewhat frequent basis in the summertime. It seems Grandpa Boris got home early on that fateful afternoon, and when he looked out the kitchen window, he saw Grandma Sweenie lying on her back on top of her favorite picnic table with Seth on top of her, vigorously moving up and down. Grandpa Boris grabbed his shotgun, opened the door and started yelling just as the love making reached its climax. Grandma Sweenie and Seth took off running naked with Grandpa Boris chasing after them with his shotgun, and after a few steps, he shot them in the butt with buckshot. He must have thought that would keep Grandma Sweenie off her butt, but instead she had a massive heart attack and died as she reached the sidewalk in front of her house. Seth continued running naked with Grandpa Boris chasing him with his shotgun until the police stopped and arrested Grandpa Boris a few blocks later."

"Is he in jail now?"

"Yes, in city jail."

"What caused Grandma Sweenie's heart attack?"

"Well, it could have been the sex on her favorite picnic table, running away from Grandpa or getting shot in the ass by a shot gun."

"I assume it could have been all three."

"Most likely."

"Hmm, although, all things considered—not a bad way to go."

"No, I suppose not."

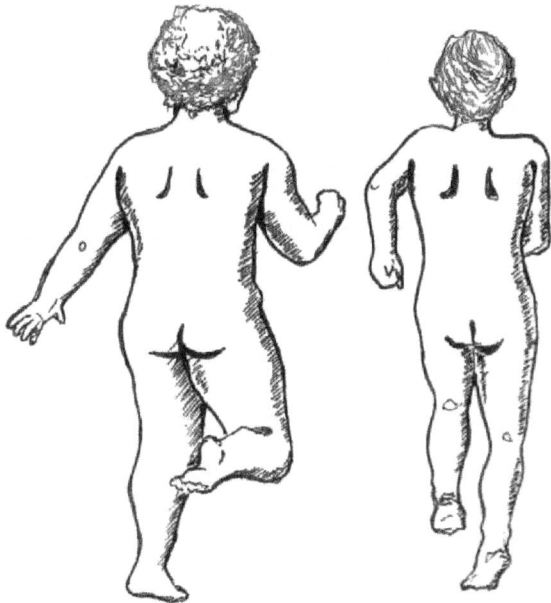

Orange

Patnude and I.M. were putting the final touches on Petty Abby before her scheduled viewing in 90 minutes at Best Funeral Home.

"Petty was certainly a large woman," I.M. commented.

"Yes, she was, and orange must have been Petty's favorite color," Patnude responded as he lightly swept the final touch of orange lipstick across Petty's lips.

Petty's hair was orange. Her dress was orange. The frames of her glasses were orange. Her necklace was orange. Her nails were painted orange. Her watch face and band were orange. She was wearing orange eye shadow. The cloth insert in her coffin was orange, and of course her lipstick was bright orange.

"Orange was Petty's favorite color. It's also mine," I.M. replied, sadly. "You know, most people called her Betty instead of Petty. She was always correcting them. I'm surprised her obituary doesn't call her Betty."

"I didn't know that orange was your favorite color. I haven't seen anything of yours that is orange," Patnude replied.

"No, I don't have anything orange. You know our profession doesn't tolerate any bold, bright colors. A silver hearse is as outlandish as we dare go. I love autumn when the leaves turn orange. I guess that is why it is my favorite season. Look at us. We always dress in dark suits, dark ties, black shoes and no flashy rings or watches. Even our cars have to be black, silver or white."

Patnude thought for a second and confirmed to himself that I.M.'s Buick was silver, his own Chevrolet was white and their hearse was silver.

"What do you think would happen if we were seen in town driving an orange car or wearing an orange sports jacket," I.M. declared. "I would love to have an orange sports jacket. It would make me feel so free and colorful. How about an orange hearse? I'm surprised Petty didn't require an orange casket, now that I think of it."

"I.M., I need to make a phone call. I think we have gotten Petty as orange as we can."

Two days later, it was I.M.'s turn to take their every-other-month sabbatical for a few days and leave Globe, where their activities were constantly being observed by the local townsfolks.

Years ago, I.M. was told this "get-out-of-town" policy from a Baptist minister who was from a small town in Alabama. His direct quote was, "You all just need to get out a town for a few days."

I.M. and Famine were driving up to Santa Fe and stopped by Best Funeral Home before leaving Globe.

Patnude looked in the rear window of I.M.'s Buick and pointed towards a sports jacket hanging from the rear seat hook.

I.M. looked, nodded, smiled and responded, "It's a gift from Famine."

Famine looked at Patnude, winked and smiled.

Patnude grinned, nodded and touched I.M. on his shoulder as the silver Buick left town.

The sports jacket hanging in back of the silver Buick was the brightest orange Patnude had ever seen.

Patnude Thinks About Getting A Personalized License Plate

I.M. took a couple extra days off on his and Famine's getaway to Santa Fe. It was late morning when he walked into Best Funeral Home's office wearing his new orange sports jacket. Patnude was on the phone. I.M. listened, as was his normal habit.

"What don't you understand? You spelled Petty Abbey's name wrong on her headstone."

"Yes. Abbey is spelled A-B-B-E-Y. That is correct. You spelled Petty, her first name incorrectly."

"No, it's not Betty, it's Petty."

"I know you spelled Betty correctly. I agree with you, but the deceased's first name is Petty, P-E-T-T-Y."

"You spelled Betty on the headstone. Her name is Petty. What don't you understand? Look at the order form from us. Her name is Petty. I printed it out myself. I'm looking at my copy of the order form."

"On your copy of the order form, the P is a B."

"Well, on my original copy it is a P. Someone in your office must have converted the P to a B."

"It looks original to you. Nevertheless, her name is Petty and you need to correct her first name."

"No, the family won't accept Betty, and they won't accept the headstone if you try and fill in the lower portion of the B with putty or something. Should I be talking to the manager?"

"Oh, you are the manager."

"Correct the headstone."

"Yes, her first name is Petty. P-E-T-T-Y. Let me know when the headstone is finished and ready for delivery and installation at Petty's gravesite at Forever Restful Cemetery." Patnude sighed to himself and hung up.

"Hello, I.M. How was Santa Fe? Have a good time? You are wearing your new orange sports jacket."

"It was great. I wore my new bright orange sports jacket every day while in Santa Fe. It is my best gift ever. I look good in orange. Anything happening, excluding Petty's headstone?"

"No. Only one funeral. Prisma Magic fell off the roof of his house directly onto his head and died instantly."

"What was Prisma doing on his roof?"

"Finishing off a bottle of tequila, which, by the way, survived the fall with a little tequila still left in the bottle."

"Too bad, I always liked Prisma. Good roofer. He re-roofed my house several years ago, although I suspected he was drinking while he was up on my roof."

"Are you going to wear your new orange sports jacket in town?" Patnude asked.

I.M. smiled and shook his head no. "I'm taking it off now. Famine is picking up her new car today. She wouldn't tell me what it is, but she was awfully excited and promised to stop by this afternoon and show it to us."

It was almost 5:00 p.m. when Famine walked into the office of Best Funeral Home. Patnude thought for a large woman she looked quite attractive. She was wearing a bright orange sleeveless dress and had her normal happy expression on her face. She hugged I.M. tightly and kissed him on each side of his face.

"Come see my new car."

"Is that a new dress?" I.M. asked.

Famine grabbed I.M. and Patnude's hands and pulled them out to the parking lot.

"Well, I'll be damned," I.M. exclaimed.

The 3 of them were looking at a bright orange Mini Cooper S Coupe.

"I love it," I.M. almost shouted. "I can't wait to wear my new orange sports jacket in it the next time we go out of town."

Patnude knew Famine selected the color orange to please I.M. He walked to the rear of the Mini and pointed to the personalized license plate. It read, "IT SHRNK."

"Very clever. I've been thinking of getting a personalized license plate for my white 4-door Chevrolet Impala," Patnude announced sheepishly.

Both I.M. and Famine gave him a questioning look.

"We need to talk about this," I.M. ordered.

"I was thinking "UR NEXT" would be the perfect personalized license plate for a mortician," Patnude replied.

I.M. gasped, and Famine winked and smiled at Patnude.

Coffee, Sissie and Eternal Life

Patnude decided he needed a break from the funeral home. It was a little after 2:00 p.m. on Wednesday, and he wanted a cup of coffee and maybe a muffin. He walked down to the Copper Nugget on Broad Street.

When he walked in, he saw Sissie Muldoon sitting at a table in the back. She saw Patnude and waved at him and motioned for him to join her.

"Hi, Sissie. How are you?"

"I'm fine. Please sit down."

"Thanks, I will. Why are you alone? Where are Rob, Robbie and Robert?"

"I broke up with them. All they were interested in was sex," she laughed and winked with her right eye. "Okay for a while, but none of them were smart enough to get out of the rain."

As Patnude ordered his coffee and bran muffin, he studied Sissie, casually of course, who set her book down.

Sissie was wearing a sleeveless, dark blue dress. It was cut short exposing most of her long legs and the front was low-cut as a fair portion of her breasts were exposed. Since Grandma Muldoon's funeral she had her mousy brown hair cut into a cute page boy style. Her lipstick was a sexy glowing pink.

Patnude understood why all Rob, Robbie and Robert were interested in was sex with Sissie. Patnude was having similar thoughts.

The waitress served Patnude his coffee and bran muffin.

"Sissie, are you still healing from your grandmother's unexpected death?"

"I'm fine. I'm over Grandma's death. We have Grandpa out on bail until his trial, and the charges have been reduced to unlawful discharge of a gun in town."

"What are you reading?"

"Eternal Life! It Can Be Yours!"

"Wow! If true, that would put me out of a job and career. Eternal Life, that is frightening to a mortician."

"I have only read the first three chapters so far."

"Do you know the author's secret yet?"

"No. I suspect his secret will be told in the last chapter."

"What do you think the secret is?"

Sissie gently touched Patnude's left hand with her right hand and motioned him to lean across the table. She whispered into his right ear, with her lips almost touching his ear, "Don't die. It's that simple. If you don't die, you will have eternal life."

"Sissie, you know the secret to eternal life. You do not have to finish the book."

"Oh I will, because I bet the last chapter will have his real honest and sincere advice. Most likely it will be, 'Buy this book's sequel which will answer all of your questions on your new eternal life.'"

Sissie continued to rest her right hand on Patnude's left hand. Neither one moved their hands.

"Why don't we go out for dinner tonight? Dutch treat. You can pick me up at 6:45. I won't have time to change since I work until 6:30. I have to get back to work now. On second thought, I won't finish the book. Here's *Eternal Life! It Can Be Yours!* You read it and let me know if I'm right."

As Sissie walked out of the Copper Nugget, Patnude noticed all male eyes were looking at Sissie, including his. He confirmed to himself this was one of his better, or maybe best coffee break ever.

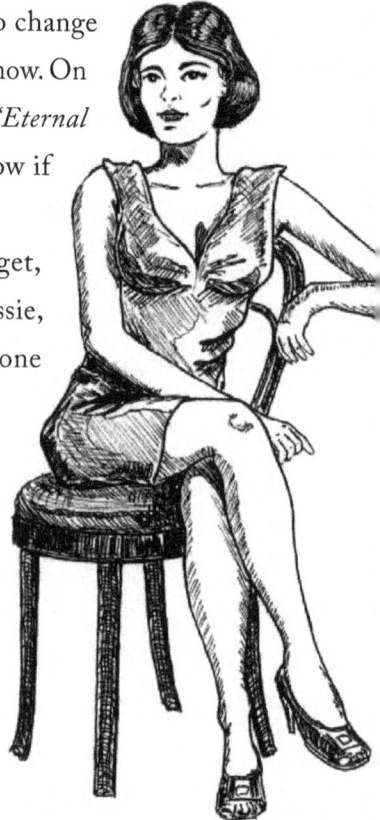

Discovering the
Young Grandma Sweenie

S issie asked Patnude to help her write a story about her Grandma Sweenie's life. She planned on doing it in 10-year installments starting when Grandma Sweenie was 20. They were in Grandma Sweenie's office hideout room, in Grandpa Boris' and Grandma Sweenie's house. Sissie was going through a banker's box of records, photos, documents, articles, etc. of Grandma Sweenie. Grandpa Boris had only been out of jail on bond for a few days and was in the living room sleeping while watching his favorite afternoon TV show.

"Patnude, I want Grandma remembered for more than having sex on her backyard picnic table with her old high school boyfriend, Seth Ostler, and then running naked with Seth and Grandpa Boris chasing them with his shotgun, then getting shot in the ass with buckshot, then having a heart attack and dying on the edge of her lawn."

"Not a bad ending, Sissie. I see a lot worse ways to depart our world."

"I know, but look this is a picture of Grandma a few years after she graduated from high school. Attached is an article that was in the *Mountain States Telephone and Telegraph* employee newsletter. Isn't she cute and a little sexy? She is wearing capri pants, sleeveless top, flat shoes, and her hair is in a ponytail. She looks so sweet, although I'm not sure about innocent. Let me read the article to you."

"*Sweenie Zobel is a resident of Globe, Arizona. She has made Globe her home and will continue her career with the Mountain States Telephone and Telegraph Company. Sweenie was promoted to senior billing clerk last January. She likes fashion, shopping, reading and dating. She graduated from Globe High School in June 1970. Sweenie was in the upper 25% of her graduating class and specialized in business classes. She currently lives with her grandparents here in Globe, but hopes to get her own apartment or even a house in the near future. Sweenie is currently dating Boris Muldoon and*

Seth Ostler, old high school friends. She says she is not ready to settle down yet. 'I like my freedom' is one of Sweenie's favorite statements."

"Certainly sounds like my Grandma Sweenie. This is a perfect start for my Grandma Sweenie story, although I'm not sure I like Seth Ostler in the article, if you know what I mean."

Discovering the Married and
Mother Grandma Sweenie

S issie continued going through the bankers box of Grandma Sweenie's records, photos, documents, articles, etc.

"Oh look, a sexy photo of Grandma Sweenie in a two-piece bathing suit. It's not a bikini, but its close and doesn't leave much to one's imagination. Let me read to you what it says on the back. 'To Boris, Baby Just Kiss Me, Love, Sweenie.'"

"Isn't that sweet and romantic?"

Patnude reached into the bankers box and pulled out a duplicate of the photo of Grandma Sweenie wearing the sexy two-piece bathing suit that Sissie was holding. He turned it over and gave it to Sissie to read.

"'To Seth, Baby Just Kiss Me, Love, Sweenie.' Well, at least Grandma treated Boris and Seth equally and didn't give either one of them this picture."

Patnude just nodded and smiled as Sissie pulled out a large manila envelope. Inside was an article from the *Globe Arizona Weekly* newspaper dated the week of August 31, 1980.

> *"Boris and Sweenie Muldoon celebrated their 10th wedding anniversary on August 15, 1980. Sweenie described the last ten years as the best years of her life, especially with a loving husband like Boris, who is the love of her life. The couple will spend their anniversary honeymoon in Phoenix at the Arizona Biltmore Hotel, while their daughter, Brendie (who turned 10 on August 28th), will stay with relatives in Globe. Sweenie thanks everyone for the anniversary cards and flowers, and especially her boss at Mountain Bell, Seth Ostler, for giving her time off from work to celebrate her 10-year wedding anniversary."*

"It appears you are going to have to do some editing with Grandma Sweenie's life to eliminate Seth Ostler, and after all, he was at her funeral and Boris wasn't."

Sissie gave Patnude a frustrated look and responded, "Grandpa Boris couldn't be at her funeral since he was in the Globe City Jail for shooting Grandma Sweenie and Seth in the ass with his shotgun."

Discovering Grandma Sweenie
as a Grandmother

It was late afternoon and Sissie and Patnude were still in Grandma Sweenie's office hide-out room. They continued to rummage through one of the endless bankers boxes of records, photos, documents, articles, etc. belonging to Grandma Sweenie.

"I'm getting a little frustrated and tired. How about a glass of wine? Grandma Sweenie must have over 50 bottles in her pantry."

"That would be nice," Patnude answered.

"Red or white?"

"It doesn't matter. Whatever you grab is fine."

Sissie found a bottle of merlot in the fridge. She opened, poured and brought the bottle of merlot and two glasses of wine into Grandma Sweenie's room.

"Here's to my Grandma Sweenie: may she rest in peace and may whatever I'm going to write about her be a tribute to her life."

Patnude and Sissie clinked their glasses three times for some reason, accompanied with an almost silent laugh as they looked at each other.

"Look, here's a picture of my mother and Grandma Sweenie. My mother was pregnant with me. Oh my God, look how big her belly was."

"Is that a baby picture of you?"

"Yes, Grandma Sweenie is holding me and Grandpa Boris has his arm around her. It's dated August 15, 1990, their 20th anniversary."

"Isn't that Seth Ostler standing in the background with some other people?"

"Yes, it is Seth Ostler."

"Where is your mother?"

"My mother was always coming and going when I was a child, however she was usually going and not coming."

"Where was she usually going?"

"Anyplace but Globe and with anybody who would take her."

"Do you know where she is now?"

"Sort of, but not in Globe, that's for sure."

Sissie refilled their wine glasses and they each made a silent toast as they clinked their glasses, only once this time. Sissie opened a manila file folder labeled 20th anniversary. It had more photographs in it and an article from the *Globe Arizona Weekly* newspaper dated the week of August 31, 1990. "Grandma Sweenie saved another anniversary article and this one has a photo of them standing in their backyard in front of Grandma Sweenie's favorite picnic table."

"I suspect it was also Seth Ostler's favorite picnic table," Patnude commented.

"Oh, be quiet," Sissie smirked as she took another sip of her wine and slid closer to Patnude where their shoulders were almost touching.

"Let me read you the anniversary article."

"Boris and Sweenie Muldoon celebrated their 20th anniversary on August 15, 1990. Their anniversary party was held in the backyard of their home, Sweenie's favorite place to be in the summertime. Sweenie held her beautiful granddaughter Sissie. Their daughter Brendie was unable to attend the anniversary party since she was called out of town for an emergency business meeting. Sweenie said the last 20 years being married to Boris were the happiest years of her life. It just doesn't get any better, but she misses Boris when he is out of town on his long-distance hauls all over America. She thanked everyone for their cards and flowers, and especially her regional manager at Mountain Bell, Seth Ostler, for her recent promotion to manager of the Globe office. She looks forward to sharing many more years with her husband Boris, her granddaughter Sissie, living in Globe and continuing her career with Mountain Bell working under Seth Ostler."

Sissie slid closer to Patnude so their entire sides were touching. She refilled their wine glasses, which emptied the bottle, and turned her head towards Patnude. Merely a few inches away from his face, she said in a loud whisper, "and don't you dare make a comment about Grandma Sweenie enjoying working under Seth Ostler."

Patnude turned his head and his lips were only a few inches away from Sissie's lips. "I wouldn't dare."

"Good."

30th Wedding Anniversary and Some Bonding

Patnude and Sissie smiled as they untangled, and slowly, kind of dressed. They had most of their clothes on, the important ones at least.

"What an unexpected and enjoyable divergence. Grandma must be looking down from heaven on us and smiling at our first, eh, encounter together in her special room and on her favorite couch." Sissie kissed Patnude lovingly on the cheek several times or more as she whispered in his ear. "Why don't you get us some more wine and I will continue looking through this bankers box of stuff."

Patnude followed Sissie's suggestion and returned with another opened bottle of merlot and carefully refilled their wine glasses. They clinked their glasses as Sissie made a toast.

"Here's to many enjoyable evenings together and maybe a few mornings." Patnude kissed Sissie on the lips.

"Later, Patnude. We need to get back to Grandma Sweenie, at least for a while."

"What's in that folder?" Patnude asked.

"It looks like pictures of me. Grandma is in a bunch of them."

"Where is your mother?"

"My mother was and is pretty much always on the road. She would only return to Globe 2 or 3 times a year for a rest, and most likely money from Grandma and Grandpa until she could hook-up with another another."

"Look, a file folder labeled 30th anniversary. It has photographs and maybe another anniversary article. Another large photo of Grandma and Grandpa in their backyard in front of her favorite picnic table and note the absence of Seth Ostler. Oh wait, this other photo has me in it and Seth is in the background standing behind Grandma."

"At least he is not in the anniversary photo that was published in the *Globe Arizona Weekly* newspaper dated August 31, 2000. Look, Grandma Sweenie has her arm around Grandpa Boris and there you are standing in front between them.

How cute you were and still are."

"You are such a smoothie for a mortician. Let me read you the anniversary article."

> *"Boris and Sweenie Muldoon celebrated their 30th anniversary on August 15, 2000. It has become a tradition for them to celebrate in their backyard with friends and relatives. Their granddaughter, Sissie, is standing in front and between them. Sweenie says Sissie and Boris are the joys of her life. Their daughter Brendie is working in California and was unable to attend their anniversary party due to the ongoing urgent and confidential nature of her work. Sweenie was surprised and delighted with the new Mustang convertible that Boris bought her as a surprise 30th anniversary gift. Sweenie said Boris is the best and she will never give him up. She is pleased that she lost 20 pounds and is about the same size that she was in high school, and she loves her new blonde hair. She owes the weight loss to a new health program Mountain Bell started and the requirement her boss, Seth Ostler, implemented that they attend the evening exercise classes. Sweenie is also celebrating her 30-year anniversary with the telephone company, although she now has to do more out of town travel with her new responsibilities. Boris is no longer doing long-distance hauls and is back in Globe most evenings. Sweenie is looking forward to many more years with Boris, the maturing of her granddaughter Sissie and her continued additional responsibilities with the telephone company working for and with her old friend and mentor, Seth Ostler."*

Sissie and Patnude were sitting close together. Patnude refilled their wine glasses and looked into Sissie's eyes.

"I know. I guess I'm stuck with Seth Ostler in Grandma Sweenie's life. Until the recent Seth Ostler escapade, I never suspected anything between them. Grandma was clever and careful of course, until the last episode with Seth."

Sissie set her wine glass down leaned over and kissed Patnude lightly on the lips and said, "Now, where were we?"

40th Wedding Anniversary for Grandma Sweenie and Grandpa Boris and More Bonding

The following afternoon Patnude and Sissie were finishing a late lunch or early dinner at Patnude's favorite restaurant in Globe, Le Citron.

"I should let you order for me all of the time," Sissie said romantically as she looked into Patnude's eyes.

"Who knew a mortician could be so, so, so."

"Enchanting with delicious taste," Patnude answered.

"Let's just leave it that I enjoyed your menu selections. We need to get back to Grandma Sweenie's room since I want to gather info on their 40th anniversary, and I am aware there will not be a 50th anniversary."

Patnude kissed Sissie on the cheek as they got up from the table, and again when he opened the passenger car door for her.

"Aren't you the romantic one? Keep those thoughts for later."

Grandpa Boris was leaving the house when Patnude and Sissie pulled into the driveway.

He sort of shouted, probably more of a yell. "Hi, door's open. I have an appointment with my attorney. There may be some additional pending charges."

"Poor Grandpa, he's all alone now."

"Well he shouldn't have shot your Grandma and Seth Ostler in the ass with his shotgun."

"I know, but who would have thought Grandma would have a fatal heart attack."

"Sex followed by running fast is not a good choice for a mature person."

"I'll keep that in mind as I get older. Would you bring that box over by the couch, please," Sissie responded and directed.

Both Sissie and Patnude looked at Grandma Sweenie's couch, looked at each other, smiled at each other and slowly sat down. Sissie opened the box.

"Lots of photos of me and Grandma, a few with Grandpa, and of course pictures of Seth Ostler. Oh look, this is a rare one with me standing by my mother. I think this was the last time I saw her."

"Let me see. I think you resemble your grandmother more than your mother. You must have been popular in high school and college. Wow, you were a knockout even then. I can't believe you are still single. Were you a junior in college then?"

"No, I think I was a senior. Knockout, huh?"

"Yes, knockout then and more so now."

"Oh Patnude, you are my favorite mortician ever." Sissie kissed Patnude on the ear and whispered, "We must talk later and do other things."

"Your grandmother framed her 40-year letter from the telephone company on being a great employee and wishing her well in retirement. Oh no, it's signed by Seth Ostler."

"I told you last night I accept that Seth is part of my Grandma Sweenie's life. Look, another anniversary article in the *Globe Arizona Weekly* newspaper acknowledging Grandma and Grandpa's 40th wedding anniversary. Once again, it's in their backyard in front of her favorite picnic table. I'm on one side and my mother is on the other side, and Seth Ostler is not in the picture."

"You said this was the last time you saw your mother?"

"Yes, she took off with another another from the State Department and went to Mexico City with him. The last I heard from her was she left the State Department another another and is now married to another another who is a CEO of a Mexican pharmaceutical company. I now have a stepdad that is either a legal or illegal Mexican drug lord and my mother is finally married."

"Well, go on and read the August 31, 2010 article from the *Globe Arizona Weekly* newspaper."

"Yes sir."

"Well, read."

> *"Boris and Sweenie Muldoon celebrated their 40th anniversary on August 15, 2010. They continued with their tradition of celebrating their anniversary in their backyard, which is Sweenie's favorite place to be. Sweenie feels blessed to have her husband Boris, her daughter Brendie and her granddaughter Sissie in her life. She never wants to part from them, although Brendie is returning to Mexico City later this evening. Boris had*

her 30th anniversary silver Mustang convertible repainted for their 40th so it looks like new. Sweenie is also starting a new life since she retired from the telephone company after 40 years of service. However, Sweenie and her old manager and friend, Seth Ostler, have started a new telephone consulting business. They still continue to religiously attend their evening exercise classes three times a week. Sweenie is excited about starting a new phase in her life with her husband Boris, her granddaughter Sissie, who will be graduating from the University of Arizona next year, and her new business endeavor with Seth Ostler. She hopes the next 40 years will be as good as the last 40 years."

"Still too much Seth in Grandma Sweenie's life, but I'm getting used to Seth now."

"What about interviewing Seth regarding your Grandma Sweenie and his relationship with her?"

"Most likely we would have to do it standing up?"

"Most likely."

"Let's go. I feel like being alone with you. I don't want Grandma Sweenie watching us."

"But she did yesterday."

"I know, but one afternoon is enough, plus I want to hear much more about being a knockout."

Patnude put the box back on the shelf, grabbed Sissie's hand and pulled her up. He kissed her on the cheek and whispered in her ear, "And no—we are not going out to Grandma Sweenie's favorite picnic table."

Preparing Sissie for An Interview

Patnude worked late at Best Funeral Home and was opening the door to his apartment when he heard his phone ringing. He answered, "Hello."

"Patnude, I need your help. I don't want to be alone tonight. I have a big interview tomorrow and I'm nervous. I need you to calm me down. No sex. I just need you. Will you spend the night with me? Please?"

"See you in a few minutes. Calm down."

As Patnude was driving over to Sissie's apartment he wondered why she was so uptight. Not at all like Sissie. He'd barely touched her doorbell when Sissie flung open the door and hugged him.

"Oh, Patnude. Thank you, thank you for coming over. Four other designers and I are being interviewed tomorrow for a big design contract for a southwest chain of brokers and investment advisors. I'm so nervous. I just need you here tonight, but no sex. Can I show you what I plan to wear tomorrow?"

"Calm down and show me what you plan to wear."

Sissie held up a bright blue dress that was low cut with a short hemline, bright blue 4" spike heels and a bright blue handbag.

"Well, what do you think?"

Patnude smiled. "Great outfit for going out to dinner, dancing and back to your bedroom, but not for an interview. Let me look through your closet."

"Patnude, I thought you told me before that I looked like a knockout in this dress."

"You do, but the knockout look is not what's needed for tomorrow. Why don't you go to bed and let me select your outfit for tomorrow," as he took the bright blue dress, shoes and handbag and headed towards her closet in the other bedroom.

"You are going to choose my clothes for tomorrow?"

"Yes, I am. I dress women almost every day and never have had one complaint."

"But they are all dead."

"Nevertheless, not one complaint. Go to bed Sissie. Now."

"Yes, sir." Sissie hugged and kissed Patnude and went to bed.

Patnude spent the next hour or so selecting and prepping Sissie's interview attire for tomorrow. He wondered if she would wear it. The selected blazer and skirt needed a little brushing to remove a few spots, ironing out a few wrinkles and emptying the pockets of her blazer. Her black pumps were scuffed up and it took a while to get them up to Patnude's shine standards. He decided to sleep on the living room couch since he didn't want to disturb Sissie.

It was morning when Patnude felt someone shaking him. "Wake up, Patnude. Wake up, Patnude. How do I look? Patnude, wake up."

Patnude looked up and a very beautiful conservatively dressed woman was looking at him. "Well, how do I look?"

"Beautiful and professional."

"Oh, I don't know about the beautiful, but I agree on the professional. You are a genius, Patnude. I love you. What do you think of me wearing my glasses instead of contacts?"

"I like the intellectual look."

"It's one I have never used before. I have always been more the T and A look."

"I know."

"Let's have breakfast and then I'm off. What did you do to my shoes? I was going to throw them out. Thank you for your shoulder strap briefcase. I can't believe how I look."

Patnude was sitting up on the couch looking at a beautiful Sissie. She was wearing a white blouse with a collar, almost like a man's shirt, a slate gray skirt that stopped at the middle of her knees, a dark blue blazer, polished black pumps with 2½ inch heels, glasses, minimal makeup, medium red lipstick, pearl earrings and a small gold watch with a black leather band. For the first time, he viewed a very attractive, professional Sissie who reeked with polish and authority. He did like the new Sissie look, however he also still liked the old Sissie look.

After a modest breakfast and several check-overs by Patnude, Sissie was ready to leave for her interview.

She kissed Patnude on the cheek and whispered into his ear. "Thanks a bunch,

I owe you big time. And don't worry—I'll go back to my provocative dresses when I'm with you."

Waiting to Hear from Sissie

It was getting to be late afternoon and Patnude was wondering why he hadn't heard from Sissie with the results of her interview. No news concerned him.

"Patnude, can you cover the entrance for me? We have a problem in Viewing Room No. 3 with Carlos Passeo," I.M. asked and stated.

"What happened?"

"His cousin, Jesus, removed Carlos' Rolex wristwatch and wedding band, and also cut his tie so he could take Carlos' diamond tie tack. Then his other cousin Jesus pulled the cut off tie with the attached diamond tie tack from the first cousin Jesus. Then, the second cousin Jesus uncoupled Carlos' gold bracelet and removed it along with his big diamond pinky ring. The first Jesus then pushed the second Jesus down and pulled the gold bracelet from his hand and ran out with the second Jesus chasing after him. Carlos' wife, Jillie, started screaming when she saw what the two Jesus cousins were doing to Carlos."

"I heard Jillie, but I thought she was just wailing over the death of her beloved Carlos."

"Nope. It was because his cousins stole all of poor Carlos' jewelry."

"Why did Jesus and Jesus steal his jewelry? Did Carlos owe them money? Was Jillie really going to bury Carlos wearing his jewelry?" Patnude asked.

"Yes, to all of your questions."

"Was the jewelry real?"

"Of course not, the Rolex was a Folex, the tie tack and diamond pinky ring were fakes, and the ring and bracelet were gold plated. Only the wedding band was gold and it was only 14K. The two Jesus cousins will be in for a real surprise when they try to sell or hock Carlos' jewelry."

"Are you going to call the police?"

"No. Jillie didn't want me to. She said it saddened her to see what Carlos' cousins Jesus and Jesus did to her Carlos. She said she will look upon the theft as their inheritance from Carlos that paid his debt in full to them. Also, they will no longer be invited to her and Carlos' annual New Year's Eve Party."

"Is Jillie still wearing one of her goofy hats?"

"Take a look and see for yourself."

Patnude peeked into Viewing Room No. 3. Jillie was standing by Carlos' coffin looking down at him and quietly speaking to him.

Her long black dress went all the way to the floor. She was wearing a straw cowboy hat with the brim painted black, the crown painted orange with black polka dots and the top removed so Jillie's long black hair could flow out of the top of it. Patnude confirmed to himself that Carlos and Jillie qualified as second generation Globe residents.

"What about Carlos?"

"I will have to put his arms back into his coffin and replace his necktie that was cut off just below the tie's knot. The viewing of Carlos is scheduled through seven tonight. I need about 15-20 minutes to get Carlos in shape to continue his viewing."

Patnude smiled to himself as he walked to the main entrance of Best Funeral Home to welcome visitors for the three viewings in progress. He knew that I.M. would use one of their standard clip-on ties as a replacement for Carlos' personal tie. He wasn't sure about the wedding band. Probably just place Carlos' right hand over his left. He thought once again how interesting the funeral business really is and he was positive that Jillie would have had to pay for Carlos' funeral in advance.

Patnude looked at his iPhone and saw he had a text message from Sissie "Meet me at Le Citron for dinner tonight at 7:30."

Dinner at Le Citron

Patnude arrived at Le Citron at 7:25 and parked his white Chevrolet 4-door Impala next to Sissie's car.

"Good evening, Patnude. Sissie is in the corner booth waiting for you. She has a new image," Mary Ellen the hostess said.

"I know, and thank you," Patnude replied as he walked towards the corner booth.

Sissie stood up when she saw Patnude. She hugged him tightly while she gave him a long passionate kiss. The two wine goblets were half full and the wine bottle was sitting on the corner of the table. Sissie still had the professional, polished, authoritative look as she had this morning.

Sissie released her hug and motioned for Patnude to sit down. She pointed to the wine goblets and picked hers up to make a toast. As usual, Sissie clinked their wine glasses more than once.

"Here's to us and to you, Patnude, my special person." Both Sissie and Patnude took a large sip of their wine.

"Well, tell me what happened?" Patnude asked, although he knew it had to be good news.

Sissie smiled as she looked into Patnude's eyes. "I was hired and beat out the four other candidates. I actually started working for Southwest Investment Brokers—or rather designing—this afternoon and work directly with the CEO, Herbie Ubber."

"I know Herbie."

"I know."

"How about some details?"

"The other four candidates, three women and one man, were dressed rather casually, and the women were showing way too much skin. I have no idea what they were thinking. Their dresses were more revealing than my blue dress that you took away from me. I was the last candidate to be interviewed. While I was sitting and waiting for my interview, I decided to act like a professional and sketched their reception area with the changes I would make. I was sketching away when Herbie walked up behind me to ask if I would join him in his office for my interview. He asked what I was sketching, and after I told him, he asked to see my sketches. I then had to walk him through my redesigned reception area. He studied it for about five minutes, asked a few questions and then hired me on the spot starting immediately. I spent the afternoon cleaning up and revising my sketch of the reception area and left it with Herbie to review."

"I'm impressed Sissie, but I knew you were good."

"Somehow your name came up. I must have mentioned we were dating or something. He said he knew you since you were a kid in Miami. He was very complimentary of you. He said you were a straight arrow and that I have chosen well, but I already knew that."

"I didn't know you were interviewing with Herbie, or I would have said something or called him."

"Do you know what else?"

"No, I don't."

"Herbie said I was on the bottom of his list of designers to interview, but he wanted to interview all of the designers in Globe. He was expecting me to be another bimbo designer. He was impressed with my professional attitude towards my design, and that I didn't waste my time reading magazines while I waited to be interviewed. Do you know what else?"

"No, I don't."

"I had to prove to Herbie that we were dating. He requested to look at my shoes to confirm that my shoes were properly shined and that the edges of the soles were also detailed. I passed his test. He commented that your grandfather, Pa, taught you the art of shining shoes."

"Very true."

"Well, let's order and eat! We'll go back to my apartment so you can help me pick some clothes for tomorrow, and then we'll go to bed early." Her glasses slid down her nose, Senator Chuck Schumer style, as she scanned Le Citron's dinner menu.

Sissie Interviews Seth Ostler

Sissie had pestered Patnude to contact Seth Ostler to arrange a meeting with him regarding his relationship with her Grandma Sweenie. Of course, Sissie was wearing one of her sexy dresses from her past T and A dress code days before she became the professional designer of today. Patnude had no choice but to accept his new assignment.

Patnude stopped by Seth's office, which just a few weeks ago was also Grandma Sweenie's office.

"Hi Seth, how are you?"

"Heartbroken and my butt is almost healed, but it is still sore and tender. I think I received the brunt of Boris' shotgun blast." Seth was standing behind a stand-up desk that looked brand new.

"Seth, Sissie is putting together a story with pictures of her Grandma Sweenie's life. She is sort of doing it in ten-year blocks. You obviously played a key role in her life. Would you make yourself available for an interview with Sissie?"

"Boris won't shoot me again, will he?"

"No, I think Boris' days of shooting people in the butt are over."

"How long will it take?"

"I wouldn't think more than a couple of hours at the most."

"Sure, I'll let Sissie interview me. We can do it in my office. Have Sissie call me to set a time."

"Thanks, Seth."

The interview was set for the following Saturday morning at ten. Sissie brought coffee and a dozen donuts, chocolate frosted cake donuts, which were Grandma Sweenie's favorite. Sissie was dressed in the old-style Sissie, which helped her to entice Patnude to accompany her to the interview.

Seth was standing up at his new stand-up desk.

"Hi, Seth, thank you for granting me this interview. I brought coffee and donuts," Sissie said.

Seth just nodded and kind of mumbled "Hi." Sissie could tell he was nervous and feeling awkward.

"Are those chocolate frosted cake donuts? They were Sweenie's favorite."

"I know. In fact, chocolate frosted cake donuts were the only kind Grandma would ever have."

Seth smiled, nodded his head and looked down at his desk. "You remind me of her when she was young. There is a strong resemblance. Your mannerisms are similar and even your voice sounds like Sweenie's. And of course, you are attractive, just like Sweenie was."

"Can you tell me about you and Grandma?"

"Hmm, let me think where to begin. We met in high school. All three of us were freshmen and we became the best of friends. I think Boris and I started dating Sweenie when we were sophomores. I don't believe either Boris or I were jealous of each other for some strange reason. Sweenie and I started being intimate the second semester of our junior year and continued until the very end. I'm pretty sure she was a virgin when we started, but it really doesn't matter."

"Did she love both you and Grandpa Boris?"

"Oh, yes. She only married Boris because he was the father of your mother. Otherwise, I believe she would have continued seeing both Boris and me."

"Did you love her?"

"Oh, yes, very much and I think even more so as we got older. I got to be with Sweenie during the day and Boris got to be with her at night. I feel sorry for Boris since I know he loved Sweenie very much and would not want to hurt her. He just got mad when he saw us on the picnic table, grabbed his shotgun and started to chase us. I think he really just wanted to scare us, which he did. I need to talk with Boris. He has to miss Sweenie as much as I do."

"I know this is a personal question, and I'm sorry for asking, but I'm wondering, where did you first have sex?" Sissie asked.

Seth smiled before he answered. "It was on a picnic table late one night at a small park the mining company owned. Sweenie wanted to repeat our original escapade and that is why we were using the picnic table in her back yard. I tried to talk her out of it, but she insisted, and you know how your grandmother could be. It was her way or no way."

"What would you do differently if you could?" Sissie asked.

"Well, probably not use the picnic table in Sweenie's backyard, but you know on second thought—probably nothing. I enjoyed and loved every minute I was with Sweenie and I know I could never change her mind once she had made it up. I did and still do love Sweenie and miss her and think of her every day."

"Thank you, Seth for telling me about you and Grandma." Sissie's eyes were tearing up as she hugged Seth.

Grandma Sweenie Looks Down from Heaven and Smiles at Sissie and Patnude

Patnude had spent the night with Sissie or Sissie had spent the night with Patnude, whichever it was, they were up the following morning having breakfast together.

"I like having breakfast with you," Sissie said as she looked at Patnude and reached across the table to hold his hand.

"Why? I don't talk; I eat my breakfast and read the paper."

"I don't know, I just do."

Patnude assumed Sissie would be working in her office today and not meeting with clients since she was wearing one of her sexy dresses and not one of her fashionable professional outfits. Patnude thought Sissie's personality changed depending on how she was dressed.

"I'm looking forward to our long weekend together in Phoenix. I can't wait to go clothes shopping. It'll be fun."

Best Funeral Home had the get-out-of-town policy for a few days every other month and this was Patnude's get-out-of-town escape with Sissie.

Sissie looked at Patnude with a dreamy-eyed look. "You know what I would like to do before we go to Phoenix this weekend?"

"I do, and the answer is no."

"You don't know what I want to do."

"I do, and the answer is no."

"You don't know."

"I do know, and the answer is still no."

"It will be safe, fun and I guarantee you will have a good time. Maybe the best ever."

"The answer is still no."

Sissie got up and sat on Patnude's lap, put her arms around his neck and kissed him lightly all around his face.

"Thursday night would be perfect since Grandpa Boris will be out of town. It will be just us."

"No, Sissie and that's final."

"Please, please." Sissie continued kissing Patnude.

"No, Sissie."

"I'll bring thick blankets. It's something I really want to do. It's important to me."

"No, Sissie. A respectable mortician doesn't do that sort of thing."

"What if you weren't a respectable mortician just for a few hours on Thursday night?"

"No, Sissie."

"We only have to do it once. That's all I ask. Please." Sissie continued kissing Patnude.

"No, Sissie. Plus, you make too much noise."

"Well, that's because of you and all the things you do to me. It's not my fault I make noise."

"No, Sissie."

"Please. It's for Grandma. It will make her happy."

"It will make Grandma Sweenie happy?"

"Yes, she will be smiling down on us from heaven."

"Nevertheless, my answer is still no."

There was almost a full moon on Thursday night and it was a little after ten as Patnude and Sissie were sort of sliding off the top of Grandma Sweenie's picnic table in her backyard. They were still hugging and kissing as they made a vain attempt to grab their clothes.

"That was perfect. I didn't make too much noise, did I?"

"No, you were passionate and discreet."

"Thank you, Patnude."

They both looked up at the almost full moon.

"Grandma Sweenie is looking down at us and smiling."

"How do you know?"

"I just know."

Later That Night and the Following Morning

Afterwards, Patnude and Sissie returned to her apartment. Sissie made a cup of hot green tea for them. They were sitting close to each other on Sissie's large green leather couch in her living room with their feet on her coffee table listening to classical music. Sissie was looking at Patnude with a quizzical look on her face.

"Why are you looking at me like that?" Patnude asked.

"I was wondering why we never met before Grandma's funeral. After all, the Globe-Miami area isn't all that big."

"I probably associate with a more responsible group than you."

Sissie smirked at Patnude and said, "You hang around with dead people. Would you rub my feet? They feel tense. Please. Thank you for not being a responsible mortician tonight. It and you were and are very special to me. I'll remember tonight forever. Wasn't it fun not being a responsible mortician for a while?"

Patnude lifted Sissie's feet onto his lap and started massaging them. When he looked up she was fast asleep.

After about 10 minutes of dedicated feet massaging, Patnude decided Sissie needed to go to bed. He picked her up and she sort of put her arms around his neck as he carried her into her bedroom. Undressing Sissie was easy since she was only wearing shorts and a tee shirt. As Patnude pulled the covers over Sissie, she mumbled "thank you for everything... don't forget my clothes for tomorrow... shine my shoes...clean up the kitchen," before she zonked out.

After Patnude completed his assigned chores for the evening, he gently slipped into bed and placed his right arm over Sissie and fell fast asleep.

"Patnude wake up. Patnude wake up. Patnude wake up. Breakfast is ready, and it is getting late."

Patnude opened his eyes and saw a professional Sissie looking at him. "You need to get up, and then let's have breakfast together. Now, Patnude."

Patnude thought this is a different Sissie this morning than the Sissie he was with last night.

Sissie took the morning paper away from him so that he would have to talk to her.

"Thank you again for last night. It was very special to me. I only wanted to do it once on Grandma Sweenie's picnic table."

"What if I wanted to do it again on Grandma Sweenie's picnic table?"

"You don't. How do I look this morning? Thanks for selecting my clothes and shining my shoes."

"You look attractive and professional."

"Thank you."

"You know sometimes I think you just keep me around for sex, selecting your clothes for the day and shining your shoes."

Sissie smiled as she answered, "Well, those are three very important reasons. I can't deny that, and I can't determine which is the most important to me. I guess it depends on what time it is. But there are also other reasons that I like you hanging around." Sissie looked down at her polished and detailed shoes and raised both legs up to admire them.

"What are the other reasons?"

"Well, let's see. You keep me warm at night. I like having breakfast with you. You carry me to bed and undress me. You take me out to dinner. You rub my feet and ankles. You give me advice. You wash my back when we take a shower together. You open and pour our bottles of wine. You listen to me. You sometimes follow my directions. The list will go on and on. Did I mention the sex? I have to run since I don't want to be late for my meeting with Herbie. I will continue my list tonight. Have a good day, my little straight arrow. See you tonight."

Sissie kissed Patnude goodbye and as she was halfway out the door, she turned around and said, "Did I mention the sex?"

Patnude smiled and nodded his head, yes.

A Weekend in Phoenix

Patnude was pleased and maybe a little excited about his four-day weekend with Sissie. They were going to Phoenix and staying at the Arizona Biltmore Hotel. This was Patnude's get-out-of-town four-day weekend that he gets every other month and his first out-of-town weekend with Sissie. He usually went someplace alone and did something touristy for four days before returning to Globe, but not this special weekend. He'd be spending the next four days with Sissie at the Arizona Biltmore Hotel.

Sissie had planned their entire four-day weekend. All Patnude had to do was follow Sissie's instructions and hang on.

They left Saturday morning for Phoenix. Patnude was a slow and careful driver, plus Sissie wanted to stop in Superior for coffee at her second favorite coffee shop. Therefore, they didn't reach the Arizona Biltmore Hotel until late morning. After checking in, they were in their room unpacking.

"Patnude put your swimsuit on."

"I thought we were going shopping first."

"No, I've changed our plans. First a quick swim, then return to our room to fool around before lunch and then we are going shopping. I'll be at the pool. Put your swimsuit on now."

Patnude liked the change in plans as he rushed to get into his swimsuit. Needless to say, they got a late start for Saturday afternoon shopping and decided to skip lunch and have a bigger dinner instead.

Sissie's first acquisition was a dark blue suit that included a skirt and pair of slacks. Patnude found her a medium grey sport jacket that Sissie could use as an alternate with her dark blue skirt and slacks. Since the stores were closing, Patnude and Sissie returned to their room at the hotel.

"What're our plans now?" Patnude asked.

"I'm going to model my new clothes for you, and then we'll go back to the pool before dinner. There's entertainment in the lounge, so after dinner we could have a drink, maybe some dancing, maybe have another drink, come back to our room, and take a late-night swim before bed. The stores don't open until noon on Sunday and I want to be there when they open."

"Any sex?"

"Maybe tomorrow morning between 8:45 and 9:00, I'll see if I can fit it in."

Patnude began kissing, massaging and hugging Sissie.

"Not now, we are scheduled for 8:45 tomorrow morning. Not now. No, not now. Okay, just this once for you, we can be off schedule," as Sissie pulled Patnude onto the bed.

Patnude appreciated Sissie's flexibility with her schedule.

Patnude and Sissie were up bright and early on Sunday morning, and by noon they were at Scottsdale Fashion Square Mall when the stores opened. They spent all afternoon shopping. Patnude made several trips to his white 4-door Chevrolet Impala with Sissie's new wardrobe. Sissie shopped until the stores closed. Patnude insisted that she must try on every garment she bought, excluding, of course, bras and panties.

"Let's stop for dinner. I'm hungry," Sissie ordered and stated.

Patnude selected a restaurant on Camelback Road. He ordered a bottle of Sissie's favorite wine, Chateau Ste. Michelle Chardonnay. As usual, Sissie made her standard toast, "To us." She then clinked her glass three times with Patnude.

"What's in the bag?" Sissie asked.

"What's in your bag?" Patnude asked.

"I bought you a gift," Sissie said as she handed the bag to him.

He slowly opened the bag.

"Come on, open the bag," she ordered.

Patnude held up a solid dark red tie and a solid blue tie.

"Thank you, these will go with my grey suits."

"They are mortician ties," Sissie explained.

"Open your bag now," Patnude ordered Sissie.

"I will. It's a box. What is it? Oh my gosh, it's a shoe shine kit. You got me a shoe shine kit."

"I did. It's something you need. Remember you have to keep your shoes shined now that you are the new Sissie."

Sissie held and looked fondly at her shoe shine kit in its box. She got up and walked over to Patnude's side of the table and hugged and kissed him a bit passionately.

"Not here, Sissie. We are in a restaurant, plus we don't have any sex scheduled until tomorrow morning before breakfast."

"I know when it's scheduled, but thank you, thank you. This is the best present ever and only you would give me a shoe shine kit." Sissie kissed him again before going back to her side of the table.

"You know that shoe shine kit is really a gift to yourself since it is your responsibility to keep my shoes shined, but I still love it."

Sissie insisted she finish the wine before they left the restaurant. She drank most of the Chateau Ste. Michelle Chardonnay.

"I'm a little tipsy," she said as she entered their room. "I think I will lie down for a while," which turned out to be all night. Patnude sort of woke her around 9:30.

"Do you want me to undress you?" he asked.

"Yes, that would be nice."

Sissie sort of helped, but the main responsibility fell upon Patnude.

Sissie woke up around 7:30 a.m. and gently woke Patnude as she whispered into his ear, "Wake up, it's Monday morning and sex is scheduled for the next hour. Wake up."

"I have to pee."

"Go pee and come back to bed," Sissie ordered.

Patnude and Sissie were only about a half an hour late from the stores opening. They shopped until about 6:00 p.m. with an emphasis on shoes today. Upon returning to their room, Sissie once again had to model all of her clothes and shoes for Patnude's final approval and of course, for both of their enjoyment. Dinner was at the Arizona Biltmore Hotel.

"Patnude, this has been a special weekend for me. I hate to see it end. You, my new clothes, new shoes and staying at the Biltmore—I could get used to this. I don't know if I'm ready to return to Globe tomorrow afternoon, but I guess I'll have to."

"There will be other four-day weekends. This is just the start."

"I know, plus I have my new shoe shine kit that I can hardly wait for you to use. Let's change into our swimsuits and sit by the pool and relax, and maybe have a drink before we go to bed."

Which they did.

Tuesday morning Patnude and Sissie just hung around the hotel relaxing before checking out and heading back to Globe. Patnude's white 4-door Chevrolet Impala was filled with Sissie's new professional wardrobe, her new shoe shine kit and Patnude's two new ties.

Sissie made Patnude stop in Superior for coffee at her second favorite coffee shop. The one in Globe was her favorite. As they entered Globe, they both had the same thought; this was a weekend they will remember forever. Sissie leaned over and kissed Patnude on the cheek.

"What's that for?" he asked.

"Because I can and I wanted to," Sissie answered.

Sissie Interviews Grandpa Boris

Sissie had arranged the Tuesday evening meeting with Grandpa Boris. It was early fall and the weather was more than pleasant in Globe, Arizona. Of course, Patnude was in attendance as mandated by Sissie. Grandpa Boris had agreed to be interviewed for her story on Grandma Sweenie and wanted to help. Grandpa Boris had two large photo albums sitting on the dining room table when Sissie and Patnude arrived. He looked good and at peace with himself.

"Grandpa, congratulations on the outcome of your trial, I'm glad all that stuff is over."

"Me too. Would you like coffee or your grandmother's favorite wine?"

"Let's have some wine," Sissie replied.

As Grandpa Boris was pouring three glasses of wine he said, "Let's go out back to Sweenie's favorite picnic table. It is probably the most appropriate place for my interview."

Sissie looked at Patnude and mouthed, "It's also our favorite picnic table," who smiled back and nodded his head, yes.

"Tell me about you and Grandma," Sissie said.

"I loved Sweenie since we first met in high school. She, Seth and I became the best of friends. I believe Seth and I started dating Sweenie when we all were sophomores. For some strange reason, I don't believe Seth or I were jealous of each other. I don't know why. Sweenie and I became intimate in the second semester of our junior year and continued until the very end. I'm pretty sure we both were virgins when we started, but it really doesn't matter."

"Did she love both you and Seth Ostler?"

"I think so. I think she married me because I got her pregnant with your mother. Otherwise, I believe she would have continued seeing both Seth and me."

"Did you love her?"

"Oh yes, very much and I think more as we got older. In reality Seth got to be with Sweenie during the day and I got to be with her at night. I never wanted to hurt or harm Sweenie or even Seth for that matter. I just got mad when I saw them on this picnic table that afternoon and started to chase them as they took off running when they saw me with my shotgun, and it went off accidentally. I just wanted to scare them, which I did, causing Sweenie to have a heart attack. I'm so sorry. I should talk with Seth, he has to be very sad and lonely as well. I should also apologize for shooting him in the butt with my shotgun."

"Did you hear from my mother regarding Grandma's death?"

"No, I didn't. The only reason Brendie would care is if there was an inheritance for her, which there isn't."

"May I ask you a personal question?"

"Sure, go ahead."

"Where were you and Grandma first intimate?"

Grandpa Boris was quiet for a few seconds while he thought.

"It was on a picnic table. Not this one, but one at a small park the mining company owned. It was late at night and everyone had gone to bed, except for the two of us."

"What would you do differently if you could?" Sissie asked.

"Probably nothing, except for keeping a loaded shotgun in the house and coming home early that afternoon. Otherwise, nothing else. I still love Sweenie and miss her every minute of the day. She always brought me happiness every day that we were together. Just thinking about Sweenie makes me happy. You know, in many ways you are very much like her when she was your age."

"Would you meet with Seth if I set up a meeting?"

"No need for that, I'll call Seth tonight."

Sissie hugged Grandpa Boris tightly as tears rolled down his cheeks.

"I love you, Grandpa."

"What an interesting story," Patnude said to Sissie as they were driving back to her apartment.

"Your Grandma loved two men her entire life and maintained a close relationship with both of them. They both knew of each other and they both loved your grandmother and continued their relationship. It's quite a story for Globe,

Arizona. You don't have another lover, do you?"

"No, I don't, and I don't want another lover. I have the one I want."

"What about Rob, Robbie and Robert at Grandma Sweenie's funeral?"

"Oh, just old friends. You aren't jealous, are you? Oh, I bet you are." Sissie leaned over, kissed Patnude on the cheek and whispered, "You will always be my number one lover."

"Thank you, I intend to be your number one, and only lover."

"You know what else is strange or unusual?"

"No, I don't."

"We both were raised by our grandparents and not our parents. Fascinating that we found each other."

Carmine Selects a New Coffin

I.M. and Patnude were sitting in I.M.'s office at Best Funeral Home when the phone rang.

"Hello, Carmine. How are you?" I.M. winced after he asked the question.

Six minutes later I.M. responded. "Two this afternoon will be perfect. Patnude will be pleased to meet with you. Goodbye."

"Was that Carmine Rightful?" Patnude asked.

"Yes, it was Carmine Rightful. She wants to revise her coffin selection and funeral arrangements."

"Oh no, that will take weeks. The last revision took over three weeks. All Carmine does is talk and talk and talk. She can't answer a question with a simple answer. "Yes" or "no" is not in her vocabulary. I once asked her what the time was, and she went on for 15 minutes. She talked about time zones, changing time in the spring and fall, having to change her clocks when there was a power failure, especially if she forgot to change the backup batteries, the watches she owns, the one she is wearing being her favorite and who gave it to her, and then she started into how she doesn't have enough time in the day to get everything done. She never did tell me what time it was. I guess the good thing with a 2:00 p.m. appointment is she won't be able to go past 5:00 p.m. because she will need to eat, and she must eat on schedule. Don't ever ask her anything about food. Oh my God, there will be no end to her babbling. Will you be here?"

"No, I have an appointment at two outside of the office." Patnude knowingly smiled as he nodded his head.

Carmine arrived at the Best Funeral Home at 1:50 p.m. Carmine was a large overweight woman. Her dress was sleeveless and bright red, and it hung over her body like a large tent. Her shoes were the old style, maybe they are back in now, black and white Converse athletic shoes. Her smeared red lipstick was a perfect match to the color of her dress and dyed bright red hair. Her voice matched her appearance, loud and showy.

"Carmine, how nice to see you. Let's go into the conference room. Please follow me. Can I get you something to drink?"

"Like, what do you have? I can't have coffee or tea this late in the day. Although, sometimes I can drink iced coffee in the afternoon, but certainly not every day. Carbonated soft drinks give me gas, plus they are too sweet, even the non-sugar drinks. I could probably drink fruit juice.

Like, prune or cranberry, but not orange or grape since they are too sweet for me. A glass or bottle of cool water might be best, but not from the tap, no siree. I don't drink Globe tap water. Bottled water would be fine. What brand of bottled water do you have?"

"Costco bottled water."

"Costco! I would think you would have a more exclusive brand. But, okay, I'll have a Costco bottled water. I will take two bottles, but only loosen the cap on one bottle and don't take its cap off."

"Here are your two bottles of water and the one on your right has the cap loosened."

"My right or your right?"

"Your right. Now can we begin on what changes you want to make to your pre-planned funeral arrangements?"

"Well, Patnude, I have been thinking. I want to look petite in my coffin. I was planning on a significant weight reduction, but I seem to be going the other way. Therefore, I thought a larger coffin would make me look more petite."

Patnude's first thought was a boxcar wouldn't make Carmine look more petite. He started tapping his fingers on the yellow legal pad on his desk as Carmine continued, "I don't think anyone would notice if I was lying in a larger coffin since they would be focusing on me and not my coffin. I do not want my feet exposed. Bunions, crooked toes, foot rash and unattractive toe nails. In fact, I only want my upper torso exposed for viewing. That might help with the petite look that I want. I do not want the lining of my coffin to conflict with my red hair. What color do you suggest? I was thinking a pale yellow or maybe even an off-white or tan liner. My dress would be a much sharper color such as red or blue. Probably not black since that would be too depressing. I know a funeral is depressing since you are saying goodbye to a loved one forever. Or maybe hopefully, only while the viewer is still alive, since the viewer and deceased will meet again in heaven or in some cases hell. Well, I'm planning on going to heaven, so I guess those viewers who are going to hell I will not see again. I don't know of any of my friends or relatives who are going to hell. Well, then again there is my ex-husband, Kipfer Rightful. If anyone is predestined on going to hell, it's him. I know living with Kipfer for ten years was like being in hell. I don't think Kipfer would come to my funeral unless it was to confirm that I was really dead. I wouldn't mind doing a fake funeral and then rise up and start talking to Kipfer when he came to my viewing. Maybe that would give him the heart attack he deserves. I kind of like that idea. What do you think, Patnude?"

"Carmine, we can't do a fake funeral."

"No, not the fake funeral, but the larger coffin to make me look more petite. I want to look petite in my coffin. Weren't you listening to me?"

"The coffin you had previously selected is 84 inches long, 27 inches wide and 23 inches high. We can custom order caskets up to 44 inches wide, but I don't think you need a 44-inch-wide coffin."

"Let me decide what I need. If you have a tape measure, give it to me. Oh look, I'm about 22 inches wide. If I get a 44-inch-wide casket, I will have almost a foot of space on either side of me and I will look petite. I like it. Write up the new deal. Same coffin as before, but I want the 44-inch-wide model. Oh, I need to decide on the liner. I think I want pale blue and I don't want the sides all puffy and touching me. I want the liner hung tight so I have almost a foot of space on either side of me. Have you got all that Patnude? Make sure to bill me for the additional cost of the extra wide coffin. I can hardly wait to tell mother about my new coffin selection. She will be so excited. It was actually her idea, as she just told me the other day, 'Make sure you will fit comfortably in your coffin since you will be spending a lot of time in it.' My mother can be a real card when she wants to be, but I guess most mothers can. At least I would think so. Is your mother a card? Okay, probably not since you are a mortician and everything is so serious to a mortician. I bet morticians almost never smile."

Carmine then pulled a stuffed black, tan and white cat out of her large tote bag. "Can I take Rinny with me? I've had her since my mother gave her to me when I was 10. Rinny's real and formal name is Rin Tin Tin."

"Yes, you may as long as there is room in your coffin."

"Derwood Sloan was the taxidermist I used to stuff Rinny when she died. Derwood is no longer around since he closed Derwood's Shoe Repair and Taxidermy," Carmine said as she stuffed the stuffed cat head first into her tote bag.

Patnude noticed Rinny, or more formally, Rin Tin Tin was missing her left glass eye. He knew not to ask any questions about Rinny. He did wonder for a second if Rinny's missing glass eye was lying in the bottom of Carmine's tote bag.

Just then the clock struck 5:00 p.m. and chimed five times.

"Oh my, look at the time, its 5:00 already. Oh, where does the time go? I have to go eat if I want to stay on schedule. Process my revised order and bill me for the additional costs. See you later. It's dinner time. Bye for now."

As Carmine left and closed the office door, Patnude had a very large mortician smile on his face.

Clyde C. Clyde's Final Thrilling Ride

Patnude was on duty late Friday afternoon at Best funeral Home. There was a viewing in process for Jasper Cohall, a long-time Globe resident and former one-term member of the Globe City Council. Jasper was sort of a celebrity in Globe and there had been a small but steady stream of viewers paying their respects all afternoon.

I.M. was at the Cobre Valley Regional Medical Center picking up the body of Clyde C. Clyde, who died a natural death after driving his all-terrain vehicle off the edge of a mountain trail and falling almost 40 feet. He was wearing a seat belt and still sitting on his all-terrain vehicle when his body was found. Unfortunately, when he drove off the trail he broke several softball size rocks free that hit him on the head. The coroner wasn't sure which killed Clyde: the fall or the falling rocks. It was probably the almost-empty fifth of vodka in a plastic bottle they found in the all-terrain vehicle's saddle bag that really killed Clyde C. Clyde. He was 60 years old and well known for combining vodka with thrilling all-terrain vehicle rides.

Patnude's cell phone rang. It was I.M. calling.

"Patnude, I need your help right now. Some idiot ran the red light and ripped the back of the hearse off and poor Clyde C. Clyde is lying along Route 60 still strapped to his stretcher."

"Is he covered?"

"Most of him is covered."

"Are you okay?"

"I'm fine. Just a little tense with Clyde lying alongside the highway. Several people are standing around looking at him and asking if there's anything they can do to help him. I called Famine and she is on her way to relieve you. Take her Mini and pick us up."

"Will you and Clyde fit in her Mini?"

"I think so, but it will be tight."

"Okay, I'll be there as soon as Famine shows up."

"Bring extra sheets to keep Clyde fully covered."

As Patnude hung up, Famine walked into Best Funeral Home.

"Here are my keys, or monitor or whatever you call them these days," Famine said.

"There is only one viewing this afternoon in the main viewing room for Jasper Cohall. There will be mourners coming in all afternoon. See you later," Patnude replied.

Patnude jumped into Famine's bright orange Mini Cooper S and headed south down U.S. Route 60 looking for I.M. and Clyde C. Clyde. He thought I.M. should be happy since orange is his favorite color and he really would like to have an orange hearse, but of course a little bigger than the Mini.

It only took a few minutes to reach the accident site. I.M. was right. The back of the silver Buick hearse was ripped off. He saw I.M. standing on the south side of U.S. 60 with Clyde C. Clyde lying on the stretcher in front of him. The sheet covering Clyde was ripped, torn and dirty. Clyde's legs from the knees down were exposed and his toe tag was flapping in the breeze. His right leg was bent towards the left. He must have broken it from his final leap and fall. I.M. was waving Patnude over. There were 10 to 15 people standing around Clyde, talking, looking and pointing at him. Patnude opened the hatch and put the passenger seat down. I.M. pulled a clean sheet over Clyde C. Clyde covering all of his body.

"I'm an old friend of Clyde's and had to carry him into my car many times when he was too drunk to walk. Can I help?" one of the bystanders commented and asked.

Two others added, "Me too, if you need help, just ask."

"Thank you, but we can manage," I.M. replied.

Patnude and I.M. picked up Clyde's stretcher and slid him into Famine's Mini. Clyde's feet were almost touching the windshield. Clyde was a tight fit. Patnude closed the hatch and the passenger's door and I.M. scrunched himself into the back seat behind Patnude and alongside of Clyde.

As Patnude was getting into the Mini he heard the one bystander that volunteered to help say to his fellow bystanders, "Wild rides were always a needed thrill for Clyde. He should be pleased if he is looking down from heaven since he is still having them."

A New Hearse for Best Funeral Home

Patnude backed Famine's orange Mini Cooper into Best Funeral Home's garage. He had to untangle and help I.M. out of the back seat. It took a minute or two for I.M. to straighten himself out.

"Oh, that's a cramped back seat, but I love the color of Famine's Mini," I.M. stated as he and Patnude struggled getting Clyde C. Clyde's body out of the Mini Cooper.

"Clyde just fit. I bet he never thought his next to last ride would be horizontal in a Mini Cooper. But if you knew Clyde, you'd know he would have approved and that he'd have had a big smile on his face."

Patnude pulled the sheet back that was covering Clyde's face to see if he was smiling. "Look at this I.M., Clyde does have just a hint of a smile."

"Well I'll be damned if he doesn't."

Patnude spent the next several hours preparing Clyde C. Clyde for his viewing the following afternoon. I.M. relieved Famine from her greeting duties and returned her orange Mini Cooper to her.

After Best Funeral Home closed for the day, Patnude was sitting in I.M.'s office. They each were drinking a bottled water, Costco brand of course.

"What are we going to do about a hearse? The Buick is toast and I don't think Famine will always be able to lend us her Mini Cooper when we need it?" Patnude asked.

"I don't think I could do another trip in the back seat of the Mini Cooper. I still feel all scrunched up," I.M. replied.

"It was only about 15 minutes that you sat in the Mini's back seat."

"Well, it was 15 minutes too long. I have called several funeral homes in Phoenix and Tucson to see if they have an extra hearse we could borrow or rent until we can get a replacement."

"What do you think about going a little upscale instead of another Buick or

Pontiac like you had before?"

"They don't make Pontiacs anymore. Upscale, huh, how upscale?"

"Cadillac or Lincoln would have some prestige. After all, it is the last ride for our clients."

"Cadillac or Lincoln? They could be expensive and after all, this is Globe, Arizona."

"It would give us an edge over our competition and their spruced-up minivan converted to a hearse."

"True, it would."

"What about a Mercedes Benz hearse?"

"Oh, that would be real expensive. Plus, I want to stay with an American made hearse."

"Okay, let's do a Lincoln or Cadillac then. What color? Let's not do silver again."

"Well, I know we can't do orange, although I would love it. Tongues would be wagging here in Globe if we did an orange hearse and then dressed in orange. I'd love it, but my, oh my."

"How about white with a dark grey or black interior? Let's not do silver again with a light grey interior."

"A white Lincoln or Cadillac with a dark interior. Okay, let me see what I can find. Not a bad choice."

Patnude thought how pleased he would be to be done with their silver Buick hearse.

It was Patnude's turn to open Best Funeral Home the next morning. He was surprised to see both I.M. and Famine's cars parked under the covered parking.

I.M. looked excited—well, as excited as I.M. could look. "Great news, I found us a hearse that is almost new. It's only a few months old and has less than 3,000 miles on it. Famine and I are going to El Centro to pick it up. We should be back late afternoon or early evening. We won't have to borrow a hearse and will put our new hearse to use tomorrow morning."

I.M. and Famine took off in her orange Mini Cooper with I.M. driving. His orange sports jacket hung in back.

Patnude wondered all day what kind of hearse I.M. was buying. He was hoping it would be a Lincoln or Cadillac. He knew it wouldn't be a Mercedes Benz. He hoped it wouldn't be black, since black is so hard to maintain. White with a dark grey interior would be perfect.

It was just after 7:00 p.m. as Patnude was locking up Best Funeral Home when he heard and saw Famine's orange Mini Cooper pull up, followed by I.M. driving their new hearse. Patnude gasped as his mouth fell open. I.M. was driving a silver Buick hearse with a light grey interior. A duplicate of their wrecked silver Buick hearse.

I.M. waved and smiled at Patnude as he parked and exited Best Funeral Home's new used silver Buick hearse. He was superciliously wearing his orange sports jacket.

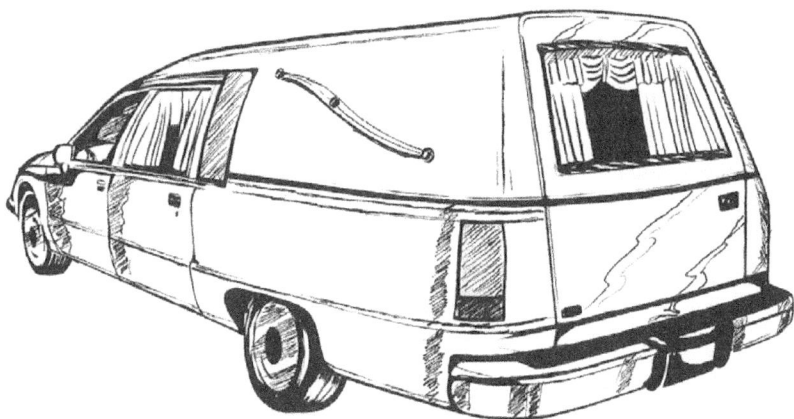

One More Thrilling Ride
for Clyde C. Clyde

Clyde C. Clyde's service at Best funeral Home was well attended. Many old timers in Globe knew Clyde and his antics, and the results of them made great gossip for many Globians.

Clyde's older brother Clarence and his older sister Claudia were in attendance. They both arrived in town the previous afternoon. Clarence was a history professor and lived in the San Diego area. Claudia was a research scientist and lived in Seattle. Both had PhDs, whereas Clyde dropped out of high school in his junior year.

Clarence and Claudia did a joint eulogy for their deceased brother.

"Clyde was the youngest and wildest in our family, and I'm sure the one who had the most fun-filled life. He died doing what he enjoyed," Clarence stated.

Claudia added, "Wild rides, vodka and accidents were my brother's trademarks. Clyde died doing what he loved. Clarence and I will miss him very much."

"We will even miss the numerous emergency phone calls from Clyde over the years when he was in trouble and needed our help," Clarence said.

"Our help was usually money," Claudia added.

"Clyde was our perpetual teenage brother. We will miss him. Thank you all for coming and paying your respects to our baby brother, Clyde."

Clarence concluded by announcing, "There will be a brief gravesite service for Clyde at Forever Restful Cemetery."

After the service for Clyde C. Clyde, Patnude and I.M. were loading Clyde's casket into the new used Buick hearse.

"I think the interior is a little darker grey than our old one," I.M. said.

"Maybe," Patnude replied.

Patnude was driving and I.M. and Clyde were passengers during Clyde's final ride to Forever Restful Cemetery.

"Let's hope this is a safe and secure ride for Clyde and us," Patnude said.

"Amen," I.M. answered. How do you like our new hearse? I know you preferred to go upscale, but this was just too good of a deal to pass up. I like the way it drives, better than our old one."

"It does drive nice. I bet Clyde would have preferred to be in Famine's Mini Cooper. It is more his style."

"Clyde probably would have, but I'm too big and old for its backseat," I.M. answered.

"I thought it was interesting, and probably appreciated by Clyde, that Clarence and Claudia each put a fifth of vodka in the coffin with him."

"Did you notice they opened each bottle of vodka and both took a swig before passing the bottles around to the guests before placing each bottle in Clyde's coffin?"

"I did, and they each rubbed a little vodka on Clyde's lips," Patnude added.

The new used Buick hearse and its occupants arrived safely at Forever Restful Cemetery. The fifteen cars that were following also arrived safely.

Clyde C. Clyde's gravesite service lasted under 10 minutes. There were over 30 of his friends and family members attending.

"I didn't realize Clyde was so popular," Clarence commented to I.M. as they walked back to their parked cars.

"I think over the years he acquired a following for all of his daredevil antics," I.M. answered.

They heard a loud boom from Clyde's gravesite as they reached their cars. I.M. and Patnude ran back to the gravesite as Clarence and Claudia followed.

"What happened?" I.M. yelled at the cemetery workers.

"The lowering brake broke and the coffin dropped six feet into the grave, but it's not damaged."

Clarence and Claudia smiled at each other, and Clarence said, "Clyde had to get one more thrilling ride. He must be smiling."

A Slow Wednesday Afternoon

It was a slow Wednesday afternoon at Best Funeral Home. I.M. and Patnude had completed all of their daily tasks and were sitting in I.M.'s office having a cup of hot tea. They weren't wishing for someone in Globe to die, but a death in the community would be good for business since it had been almost two weeks since their last funeral and burial service.

"You know, Patnude, a funeral home is an unusual business. Our service or product is only needed when someone dies. Someone's death and their loved ones' sadness brings us revenue and, in theory, happiness with the profit that is generated."

"I know, but we do provide a valuable service to the loved ones in their time of need, and don't forget—the goal of life is death."

"I know all of that. But sometimes I wish this was a more fun business where people liked to see and be seen with us. Where everyone was happy and smiling, instead of being sad and crying."

"Well it isn't a happy business. We don't bring joy to people. However, I guess we could restrict our service to accepting only the deceased that everybody wished were dead, like ex-somethings, and then our funeral service would be a time of celebration."

"We would starve to death. There is always someone out there that would miss them."

"I know. You are so right."

There was a light knock on I.M.'s office door. A police officer stuck his head in and spoke, "Excuse me I.M. and Patnude, I have a matter I need to discuss with you if you have a few minutes."

"Sure, come on in Jim," I.M. replied.

Jim Peterson was a sergeant with the City of Globe Police Department. With him was Jesus Passeo, a cousin of the deceased Carlos Passeo. Jim and Jesus sat down. Jesus didn't look at I.M. or Patnude, he just stared at the floor nervously.

"Jim, how can we help?" I.M. asked.

"Well, Jesus says that Carlos Passeo was wearing his valuable jewelry at the beginning of his funeral service and that you removed and kept it prior to his burial. He says his cousin Jesus will back him up."

"Let me understand Jesus' claim. He is saying that we removed Carlos' jewelry before he was buried and then kept it. That's theft isn't it?"

"Yes, it is. Jesus says he won't press charges if you return the jewelry to him or pay him the fair market value of Carlos' valuable jewelry."

"Why wouldn't we pay Carlos' widow Jillie if we stole his jewelry?" Patnude asked.

"Because Carlos owed Jesus and his cousin Jesus almost $20,000."

Jesus nodded his head and said, "It was actually more than $20,000."

How valuable was Carlos' jewelry?" Patnude asked.

"Jesus says over $20,000," Jim answered.

I.M. looked at Patnude. Both were smiling.

"Twenty thousand dollars is a lot of money," Patnude said. Would Jesus accept less not to file any theft charges against us?"

Jesus was quiet and sort of smiled as he said, "Maybe $15,000 as there would be selling expenses for the jewelry."

"Before we pay $15,000 to Jesus I would suggest we look at something first," I.M. said.

Jesus was still smiling.

Patnude was fooling around with his computer for almost five minutes before he announced, "I found it. Jim and Jesus, you might want to watch this video. It is not very long."

Jesus' smile vanished as Jim and Jesus watched the video of Jesus and his cousin Jesus removing Carlos' jewelry from him as he lay in his coffin, Jesus grabbing Carlos' gold bracelet from his cousin Jesus, then both of them running out of the viewing room and Jillie screaming. "Would you like to view it again?" Patnude asked.

"I would like a copy of it. Would you send it to me?" Jim requested as he gave

Patnude one of his cards. Jesus got up to leave and Jim stopped him. "Jesus, you need to come down to the station with me," Jim said as he cuffed Jesus. "Sorry I.M. and Patnude. Thanks for the video."

After Jim and Jesus left, I.M. and Patnude were back sitting in I.M.'s office and sipping their now-cold tea.

"A little excitement for a quiet afternoon. I guess Jesus missed the security cameras," Patnude stated.

"He must have been desperate and not too clever, which he proved by loaning $20,000 to Carlos."

"I will call Jillie and tell her what happened. How much did the security cameras cost?" Patnude asked.

"I think the complete system, inside and outside was about $15,000 to $20,000."

"I guess so far about a break even, but of course we still have the system."

"Well that would be one way to look at it."

The Accidental Death of Rolfer Sharper

As usual, Patnude was driving the new used Buick hearse and I.M. was riding. They were headed to the medical center in Globe to pick up the body of Rolfer "Rolf" Sharper. Rolf was in his late 30s when he died.

Late two nights ago he was riding his trail bike without any lights on a copper mine pit road, and he was run over by a huge mining truck. It was almost midnight when Rolf met his fate with the huge mining truck driven by Rodney Nail, who ironically purchased a used car three weeks before from Rolfer Used Cars. Rumor had it that Rodney was unhappy with his new used car, which frequently was the case with Rolfer Used Cars customers.

It wasn't until sunrise the following morning that Rolf's squished and flattened body was discovered.

"I anticipate Rolf's funeral will be a closed casket funeral," I.M. said to Patnude.

"I couldn't imagine it could be anything different. Probably embalm, bag and close the coffin is all we will have to do. Maybe put a picture of Rolf on top of the coffin. He always dressed the same since I have known him."

"How did he dress?" I.M. asked.

"He always wore his thick horn rim glasses and a red baseball cap pulled down low. His white long-sleeved shirt was almost always soiled. In the summer he would role his sleeves up and switch from his scuffed up brown wing tips to sandals. His khaki pants were well used and needed to be ironed. I knew him for over 20 years and that's all I ever saw him wear, even when he rode his bicycle."

"Wasn't he supposed to be smart? Like almost a genius?"

"He was in some areas, but he didn't have an ounce of common sense. He could do all math calculations in his head, never needed a calculator, nor did he wear a watch. But, he always knew the exact time and date. He knew all of the specs of his car inventory and all of his customers and their complaints."

"Did you ever buy one of his used cars?"

"No, I knew better than that. I don't believe Rolf had many repeat customers. I bet most of the mourners paying their respects to Rolf will be to ensure that he is really dead. He never had any real friends, at least that I knew of."

"How about any female relationships?"

"I never saw or heard of any serious relationships. Rolf always thought or believed he had a way with the opposite sex, but he didn't."

"None?"

"None that I ever heard of."

"How sad."

"Sissie told me about a year ago he sort of tried to pick her up when she was having lunch one Wednesday. It was almost comical in that he asked if he could buy her a drink at 11:30 a.m. on a Wednesday. It gets better since Rolf could not pronounce a word that began with S. He just deleted it. He called Sissie, Issie. It became a comedy when Sissie tried to correct him. Oh, his last name is even better. It's Sharper, but if you asked him his name, Rolf would respond and say Harper. You would respond and say Harper, and he would say no, it's Harper, and it would continue until he spelled Sharper out for you or you just gave up."

"Could he say 'S'?"

"Yes, he could. He just couldn't say it if it was the first letter of a word. Oh, this is a funny story I heard. When he was in high school he got into a fight with a girl called Sarah Ellen who beat him up. He used to say 'Arah beat the hit out of me.' It just went on and on, he would say aw instead of saw, hut instead of shut, hucks instead of shucks, lut instead of slut, Eptember instead of September and so forth. At times it was amusing to talk with him if you could get a lot of words that began with S in the conversation. The best was when something dissatisfied him he would say, 'aw, hit'."

"Almost comical."

"Do you remember when he ran for city council a few years ago? He hand painted all of his signs and then made copies of them and passed them out to would-be supporters. Oh, I remember going to one of his campaign speeches, or rather peeches and he went on and on and on about how he was going to improve our treets in Globe. We were going to have good treets if he was elected. His nose was always running and he kept wiping it during his political speeches and you could hear it through the PA system.

Rolf was a character alright. He liked to drink even and evens which was another routine to watch at a bar. He of course couldn't hold his liquor and became obnoxious after several even and evens, and by the third or fourth even and evens he sat down and fell asleep.

I only knew one female who liked Rolf, and that was Calendar Day. She always wanted to date Rolf, and he'd see her from time to time, but nothing steady or routine. Calendar is a nice, pleasant lady and I never understood what she saw in Rolf. I know he'd see her when she was ready to buy another used car from him, which was frequent since she bought a bunch over the years."

"Sounds like he will have an unusual group of mourners attending his funeral," I.M. said.

"It should be a small group, but I guarantee Calendar will be there. But you know, it's a real shame that Rolf never put his gift of intelligence to good use. It was a waste of a valuable asset."

"How did you know him?"

"He was a senior when I was a freshman at Miami High School. For some reason I talked with him, probably because no one else would. He also went to the U of A as a freshman the year that I was a freshman there. I don't know what he did those three years after graduating. Oh, I do, he decided to become a painter for his career."

"A house painter?"

"Oh no, an artist, a modern artist. I think he told me it took him a year for each painting. Therefore, he did three in three years."

"Did you ever see them?"

"Yes, once in his garage. They were large paintings, about 4 feet by 4 feet. One painting was basically red, the other yellow and the third orange. I remember he told me, 'You have to look and study my brush strokes to understand what I'm telling you with my paintings.' They looked like three large red, yellow and orange paintings to me. Maybe I should go back and actually study them."

"Who is going to pay for his funeral?"

"His parents established a substantial trust fund for him before they died. That's what he lived off of. He never sold enough cars at Rolfer Used Cars to support himself."

I.M. and Patnude unloaded Rolf's body, or what remained of his compressed body, from the hearse.

Patnude was correct. Preparing Rolf's body for the closed casket funeral was rather easy. He was able to download a picture of Rolf from the Rolfer Used Cars website to display on top of the casket. The viewing and service was scheduled for 11:00 a.m. the following day with the burial and gravesite service at 3:00 p.m.

The following morning at exactly 11:00 a.m. Calendar Day was the first mourner to arrive. Patnude didn't look at the back of her car, but he was positive it had a Rolfer Used Car sticker on it. Probably two he thought.

Calendar hugged Patnude for a long 10 seconds before she walked over to Rolf's coffin.

She asked, "Does it have to be closed?" as she pointed towards Rolf's closed coffin.

"Yes."

"Rolf always appreciated your friendship. He told me he didn't have many friends, just a few. He could be very nice to me and then go out of his way to avoid me. I don't know why, but I think I sort of loved him in a strange way. His intelligence and understanding of complicated matters used to mesmerize and overwhelm me. He was so damn smart in many areas and so incompetent in life. We made out from time to time, but never had sex. It wasn't because I wouldn't have, he just stopped after a while and got up and did something else. I will need to get on with my life now that Rolf is gone. But I will miss him."

Patnude hugged Calendar again. "I will also miss him, and yes, you do need to get on with your life."

"I know. I'm going to have to find another car dealer since it is about time for me to trade again."

Both Patnude and Calendar smiled as they nodded their heads, yes.

There were eight mourners at the service, including Calendar and four cars, each with a Rolfer Used Cars sticker on the back, except Calendar's car had two stickers. The four cars followed Best Funeral Home's hearse to Forever Restful Cemetery for Rolf's burial service.

Later that night Patnude and Sissie had a quiet dinner together. Patnude's thoughts were of Rolfer Sharper and that he would miss him.

The Sale of Rolfer Sharper's Paintings

The following morning after Rolfer Sharper's funeral, Sissie and Patnude were having breakfast together. Patnude, as usual, was quietly eating his healthful breakfast, as required by Sissie, and reading the morning newspaper, as not required by Sissie.

"I have an idea, Patnude."

"Hmm, okay. A good idea I hope. And no, we are not using Grandma Sweenie's picnic table again, unless of course…"

"Patnude! Put the newspaper down and listen to me."

"I'm listening."

"I.M. considers himself an art collector. You told me Rolfer spent three years painting three paintings. Maybe I.M. should view them and consider buying and displaying them. What do you think?"

"Not a bad idea. You're smarter than you look."

Sissie was wearing one of her T and A outfits and he knew she had to be working in her office today and not meeting with any clients. He thought he could get away with his comment, of course, he couldn't. Sissie politely removed the newspaper from him, his coffee cup, and what remained of his breakfast.

"I think it's time for my unwelcome guest to get ready to leave." Which he did after a few kisses and hugs.

Later that morning, I.M. and Patnude were sitting in I.M.'s office planning for tomorrow's funeral service and just chatting when Patnude brought up Sissie's suggestion.

"Good suggestion from Sissie. I agree I should view Rolfer's paintings. They might be unique and I could buy them from his estate. Do you know where Rolfer kept them?"

"I believe in his garage. I'll call Falls and see if we can get the keys."

"Dan Falls is doing the estate?" I.M. asked.

"Yes."

Later that afternoon, Patnude and I.M. were in Rolfer's garage.

There was an old two-tone blue Buick Roadmaster on one side of the garage. All the tires were flat. A white late model Honda Accord was parked on the other side of the garage. The three paintings were hanging on the back wall. Each painting had its own colored light, red, yellow and orange. When turned on, the lights enhanced the already bright paintings.

"How unique. They are 4 foot by 4 foot. They kind of blend and evolve from each other. I have the perfect wall in my dining room to display them," I.M. said as he approached the orange painting to study it. I.M. kept moving closer and closer to the orange painting and continued to repeat, "How interesting."

All Patnude saw were the same large red, yellow and orange paintings he viewed years ago.

I.M. moved from the orange painting to the yellow painting, to the red painting and then back again to the orange painting, continuing his revolving examination and repeating, "Hmm, how interesting."

Patnude continued to see three large red, yellow and orange paintings. "I think the old Buick Roadmaster was Rolfer's father's car. I think his father bought it new and just kept it for some reason, and Rolfer probably kept it out of respect for his father. He must have been more sentimental than I thought, or the tires were flat when Rolfer's father died and he never got around to moving it. I guess it really doesn't matter. Dan Falls will have to do something with it. What do you think of the paintings?"

I.M. now had his little keychain flashlight shining on the orange painting as he looked closely at the lit-up spot with a small magnifying glass.

"They are unique and I like them and will buy all three. They are a set and should not be broken up."

"What do you like? I don't understand."

"I believe Rolfer painted an intricate scene or object or whatever, in great detail with intricate strokes in these three paintings, but he used the same color paint for the entire painting. Therefore, one must study the brush strokes in detail to determine what Rolfer was painting. If I am right, that was what took him so long to complete each painting. It would take intense concentration to paint what you are visualizing with the same color paint. Not to mention starting and stopping.

Unbelievable. I don't know what the scenes or subjects were, but I bet the three paintings are part of a story or theme. Didn't you tell me he told you that one must study in detail the brush strokes on his paintings?"

"Yes, I did. That's what Rolfer told me."

"Let's return the keys to Dan and try and buy them now."

"Are you serious?"

"I am. I told you I have the perfect wall in my dining room to hang all three of them. It will be a challenge to see if I can determine what Rolfer painted."

While driving back to Dan Falls' office, Patnude observed I.M. in deep thought. He was pretty sure I.M. was planning his strategy to use on Dan. Both I.M. and Dan were pretty good horse traders. This could be an interesting negotiation.

Dan greeted them, and Patnude handed Rolfer's house keys to him.

"What did you think of the three paintings? Do I have a sale?"

"They are unusual. I like them and will buy all three, but of course that depends on the price."

"Are you going to keep and display them or resell them?" Dan asked.

"I never sell any of the art I collect."

"Six hundred dollars for all three."

"Sold. I would like to pick them up now. I have a wall I can display them on, and Patnude is captive labor to help me hang them this afternoon."

It was late afternoon when I.M. and Patnude finished hanging Rolfer Sharper's three original paintings on I.M.'s dining room wall. The ceiling was 14 feet high, and the three paintings fit perfectly.

Patnude could tell that I.M. was pleased and excited since he was smiling as he focused on the three paintings.

"They fit perfectly and set off my dining room. All that's left is for me to study them and determine what Rolfer actually painted."

"Do you have a favorite?" Patnude asked knowing the answer.

"I like all three, but of course the orange one is my favorite and the one I will study first."

Patnude nodded as he said, "Don't you think you should study them in the sequence Rolfer painted them?"

"Probably so, but I'm doing the orange one first."

Sissie Scrutinizes the
Three Rolfer Sharper Paintings

It was closing time for Best Funeral Home on a busy Thursday. They had two burial services and one viewing scheduled for Friday.

"Busy week. It's either feast or famine in this business," I.M. said as he was locking the doors and setting the alarm.

"I know," Patnude replied. "Have you been studying Rolfer's paintings and have you discovered what Rolfer painted?"

"Yes and no, no, no. I think I recognize something and then I lose it or it turns out to be nothing. It's a challenge, but fun."

"Still just studying the orange painting?"

"Yes, still just the orange painting. Maybe I should have Sissie look at them. She has artistic talent. In fact, why don't you and Sissie join Famine and me for dinner tomorrow night? I'll cook something on the grill. How about 6:30 tomorrow night and you can bring dessert. Sissie and Famine can study the three Rolfer paintings and tell me what they see, if anything."

"Okay, we will bring a special dessert like vanilla ice cream with chocolate syrup."

As expected, Patnude and Sissie arrived at I.M.'s house at exactly 6:30 p.m. Sometimes Patnude's precise punctuality annoyed Sissie, but not this Saturday night. Patnude had a fleeting thought that Sissie was going to accept him as he was, but then he quickly came back to reality.

I.M. accepted Sissie's desserts of banana cream pie and chocolate banana vanilla ice cream as he and Famine welcomed them.

Famine was wearing a bright orange sleeveless summer dress. Patnude thought Famine was a bit thinner, but still a large woman, and he knew the orange dress she was wearing was to please I.M.

"Ladies, I want you to look at and study my new paintings. They're hanging on my high dining room wall. The artist was Rolfer Sharper. Each is a painting of something; Rolfer used the same color paint for the entire painting. You have to study his brush strokes to determine what he painted. I've been studying the orange painting, which was his last. I sometimes think I've discovered a lead or hint about what Rolfer painted, but then it goes nowhere and I'm back to nowhere, ground zero. We'll leave you two in here with your glasses of wine to figure it out while Patnude and I grill the steaks."

Both Sissie and Famine sat quietly studying the three paintings while drinking their wine. After about 20 minutes, their wine glasses were almost empty. Famine got up to get the bottle. When she returned and refilled their glasses, Sissie announced, "I think I know what Rolfer painted."

She pulled Famine close to her and whispered into Famine's right ear. "Uh huh, uh huh, I think I see."

"Keep staring, Famine."

"I am, and I think you're right. I see it now."

I.M. and Patnude returned with four grilled steaks.

"They smell great. I'm hungry and haven't had steak in a while," Sissie almost shouted.

"What do you see now?" I.M. asked.

"Sissie and I see what Rolfer painted. It's actually pretty clear once you know what to look at."

"You do not."

Sissie replied, "We do."

"You really do?"

Both Sissie and Famine answered in unison, "We do."

I.M.'s face turned red as he stared at the three paintings. Patnude served the steaks. All I.M. saw were three large red, yellow and orange paintings.

"Tell me what you see. No, don't. I want to discover the paintings myself." I.M. continued staring at the three Rolfer paintings.

"Eat your steak before it gets cold," Famine directed I.M.

"I will, I will. Are you sure you see what he painted?"

"It's perfectly clear and the more I look the clearer it becomes."

"Really?"

"Really. Why don't Famine and I draw a rough outline of what we see in each painting along with a brief description and we will put it in a sealed envelope. That way if you get desperate you can open the envelope."

"Okay, that would be perfect, but I won't open the envelope."

"What do you see Patnude?"

"The same thing I have always seen, three large paintings colored red, yellow and orange."

After dinner, Sissie and Famine prepared their sealed, double sealed and triple sealed envelope and handed it to I.M., who was still fixated on the three Rolfer paintings.

I.M. could hardly pull himself away from his continual examination of Rolfer Sharper's three paintings to say good night to Sissie and Patnude. Famine actually had to force him to leave the dining room.

Patnude was driving his white 4-door Chevrolet Impala, heading towards Sissie's apartment. He looked over at her when he stopped for a red light and realized how much he liked, or loved, her and how lucky he felt. His thoughts went back to the time when they'd accidentally really met, had coffee together, and met again for dinner that same evening.

"I suspect I.M. is back studying Rolfer's paintings and most likely it would be the orange one," Patnude said.

"I'm sure you're right. Famine will most likely have to drag him to bed. He should be viewing the paintings from 10 to 15 feet away, not up close."

"Are you going to tell me what Rolfer painted in his three paintings?"

Sissie looked at Patnude with a loving smile and said, "Sure I will. Rolfer painted a red, yellow and orange painting."

"What else? How about the details?"

"Oh, you want to know about the details. You should have asked Rolfer when he was alive and then you would have known for sure, or you could sneak back to I.M.'s dining room and open the sealed envelope. Who knows, maybe the envelope has already been opened, but I doubt it."

"I guess your answer is no."

"Oh look, an open parking space right in front of my apartment!"

A Thursday Drive to Safford and Back

Patnude finished his coffee and was ready for his drive to Safford. He needed to pick up the body of Emerson Sparkling and bring him back to Best Funeral Home. As Patnude was getting into the new used silver Buick hearse, I.M. bolted out the back door of the Funeral Home and jumped into the hearse.

"I'm going with you to pick up Emerson's body. That woman is on a rampage this morning and just won't shut up. You would think *I work for her.*"

"What's up with Maria today?" Patnude asked.

"I used a blue pen instead of a black pen on the checks I wrote. She insists all checks should only be written with a black pen. What difference does it make? Her 4 to 12 hours per week can be pure hell for all of us. She offends everyone."

"Why don't you change bookkeepers?"

"Because she is a good bookkeeper and she is dependable. I just need to be out of the office on Thursday mornings."

"What's the story on Emerson Sparkling?"

"When he turned 37, he decided he wanted a new life. He divorced his wife of almost 20 years, quit his job at the post office after almost 20 years and became a free spirit, whatever that means. Anyway, last year he decided he wanted to be a runner, a barefoot runner. His last quest was to run up and down Mt. Graham barefoot. He made it up okay, but it was the downhill run that was his demise. He hit a patch of ice, lost control and nailed an old pine tree head first and broke his neck and died instantly."

"How old was Emerson?"

"Exactly 39, he died on his 39th birthday."

"I wonder if his family is going to put up a memorial sign for Emerson by the big pine tree like some families do for auto accident victims."

"I don't know. The family might not be allowed to since the big pine tree is on National Forest land. Most likely there are restrictions."

"Most likely."

"I think there is a good chance this could be a closed coffin viewing since Emerson hit the tree face first, but maybe we can patch him up."

"Did he ever wear shoes after his barefoot commitment?"

"I don't know for sure, but someone told me last year when we had some snow they saw Emerson slipping and sliding as he ran down Broad Street barefoot."

It took a little over an hour to reach the Mt. Graham Regional Medical Center in Safford. Since it was almost lunch time, I.M. decided they should have lunch in the hospital's cafeteria. After their hospital cafeteria lunch, they loaded Emerson Sparkling's body into the hearse.

"What do you think, closed or open coffin?" Patnude asked.

"I'll try for open, but it probably won't look like Emerson."

"Do you think many mourners?"

"Probably more curiosity seekers to see how Emerson looks after nailing a pine tree head first on Mt. Graham. Maybe some who will use Emerson's death as an example to their children of not to do stupid things."

"Oh, I forgot to tell you I saw Kipfer Rightful with his new bride in the coffee shop. Carmi looks to be about 20 years younger than Kipfer and quite attractive. Kipfer introduced me to her, and I liked her after a few minutes of chit chat. Carmine will go bonkers when she sees Kipfer and Carmi together. Carmine must outweigh Carmi by 200 pounds or more."

"Doesn't Kipfer have a burial plot right next to Carmine, whose plot is next to her father and mother's plots?"

"That's what she told me. I suspect after she sees Carmi she will be revising her funeral plans again. If she calls, make it a late afternoon appointment."

Maria was just locking up Best Funeral Home when Patnude and I.M. pulled around back. Patnude backed the hearse into the garage to unload Emerson Sparkling's body. When I.M. opened the passenger door, he heard Maria semi-yelling at him.

"I got everything up to date and there are ten checks with attached envelopes with postage on them for you to sign and mail."

"Thanks, Maria. See you next Thursday morning," I.M. replied.

"I went through your desk and threw out all of your blue pens. You only have black pens now."

"Thanks again, Maria," I.M. said as he looked at Patnude and shook his head.

Sissie Makes a Decision

After an early dinner at Le Citron, Sissie and Patnude were walking to his white 4-door Chevrolet Impala. Sissie was holding onto Patnude's arm somewhat tightly.

"Let's drive down to Miami. I want to see the hardware store where your grandparents raised you," Sissie requested.

"Okay, we can do that. But why do you want to see it now?"

"Just drive down to Miami and show me the hardware store. I don't want to do an analysis of why I want to see it now instead of later, or why I didn't want to see it before."

Patnude was learning, although slowly at times, not to over-analyze Sissie's desires or requests or orders, as he pointed his Chevrolet Impala south on Highway 60 towards Miami. It only took a few minutes to reach the closed The Complete Hardware & Variety Store on Sullivan Street in Miami.

Sissie exited Patnude's car as soon as he stopped and crossed Sullivan Street for her close examination of the old store.

"Do you have keys to the building?"

"No, I don't."

"I wonder if it is still for sale?"

"I would imagine every empty building in Miami is up for sale."

Sissie looked into the store through the old plate glass windows and saw what remained of the old hardware store's counters, shelves and nail bins.

"It's all brick construction and looks to be in good condition, two stories with living quarters on the second floor. Oh look, it has a little deck or porch in the back, although the old stairs might need some work."

Patnude looked up at the porch and thought of the many pleasant times he sat up there with Pa and Ma. It seemed almost like yesterday.

"Don't climb the stairs. Some of the wood could be rotten."

"How big were the living quarters?"

"There is a living room, dining room, kitchen, two bedrooms, a good size office and two bathrooms. There was also a deck on the roof that was reached by a pull-down staircase. Pa and Ma loved to sit up there in the evenings and stargaze."

Sissie was standing in front of a garage door at the back of The Complete Hardware & Variety Store, "How many cars can you fit in there?"

"Two, maybe three small cars."

Sissie walked around the building three times as she continued to examine the building and question Patnude about it.

"Do you know what it is worth?"

"No idea, I can't imagine very much. It probably needs a lot of work to make it useable."

Sissie gave Patnude one of her looks that suggested he didn't have a clue what he was talking about.

Later that evening Patnude and Sissie sat in Sissie's living room reading and listening to classical music.

"Let's go to bed. I'm tired and have an early meeting with Herbie tomorrow morning. You need to select my clothes and make sure my shoes are shined." Sissie kissed Patnude on the lips, just a little passionately. As she headed towards the bedroom she said, "I think we should buy the old building and recondition it. I can use the first floor as my office and we can live up on the second floor. It should make you feel like you're back home again. I'll find out what they are asking for it tomorrow. Pick out my clothes for tomorrow and get into bed. I told you it's getting late. Now get moving and close your mouth."

After the completion of his chores and trying to grasp the ramifications of Sissie's new directive, Patnude discovered a very passionate Sissie as he slid under the covers.

I.M. and Patnude
Have a Chat and a Drive

It was mid-morning and the viewing was scheduled to start at 1:00 p.m. for Emerson Sparkling. Patnude thought he and I.M. did a remarkable job with Emerson's face. He looked fairly close to his photographs, at least in Patnude's opinion. I.M. situated Emerson's body so the overhead lights were not shining on his face, and then dimmed the lights to create some shadowing. Patnude thought the deceased's final exposure to the living world had a bit of a theatrical touch to it. On second thought, maybe everything in life had theatrical touches. Patnude walked back to I.M.'s office.

"Emerson looks good. Pretty close to natural," Patnude said. "You did a good job."

I.M. poured a freshly brewed cup of coffee for Patnude.

"How are you and Sissie getting along? Are you two getting serious or whatever they say these days?"

"I think so. We're not seeing anyone else and we spend almost every night together. Come to think of it, I bet it's been over two months since we slept alone."

"I like Sissie. She is smart and attractive. Plus, she knows what Rolfer Sharper painted in those paintings that I have, even though I still can't figure them out."

"She wants us to buy my grandparents' old hardware store in Miami and rebuild, remodel and bring it up to date or whatever. She thought she could use the first floor as her office since it faces Sullivan Street."

"Hmmm, I've always wanted to open a viewing parlor in Miami. There have been some Miami residents that did not like the funeral for their loved ones to take place in Globe. It would certainly give us an advantage to have the availability of a Miami viewing parlor. If you are serious about buying the old store, I'd like to meet with Sissie and see what she can design for a viewing parlor. We have some time now—let's drive down to Miami and take a look at the building. That Sissie is a smart girl. Let's go! Bring your coffee with you. You can drive."

As Patnude drove to Miami he realized since he met Sissie a lot of decisions were being made for him. He didn't mind though, because they were good decisions.

Patnude pulled up and stopped in front of the old building that he was raised in. I.M. jumped out for his initial tour and inspection.

"Perfect location. I like it. I think it would work perfectly for our Miami location. I like it. Call Sissie and see when she's available to meet with me. You are a genius Patnude, always thinking ahead."

Patnude smiled and nodded as he thought to himself, *Genius? All I do is drive either Sissie or I.M. from Globe to Miami to look at this old store.* But he did like the plans for the potential new building.

Carmine Runs into Her Ex-Husband

Patnude met Sissie for morning coffee at the Copper Nugget. They both considered it a special treat when they could arrange their schedules to share a morning coffee. This was going to be an easy day for Patnude since there were no funerals scheduled and the new used Buick hearse was clean and polished. Patnude was walking up Cedar Street when he saw a red Honda minivan run the red light on Broad Street and broadside a new white Mercedes Benz SUV. The passenger side of the Mercedes Benz was caved in, as was the front of the minivan with steam billowing out of its hood.

Patnude saw the driver of the red Honda minivan attempt to jump out of it, but it was a very slow process. He could hear the woman starting to yell at the Mercedes Benz and its occupants. "You ran the red light, you damn fool!" she screamed.

Patnude recognized the screaming woman—it was Carmine Rightful. She looked the same as always. Large, overweight and wearing her red sleeveless tent dress, black and white Converse athletic shoes, bright red lipstick to match her bright red hair.

Patnude saw police Sergeant Jim Peterson walking towards her. "That asshole ran the red light!" she repeatedly screamed.

Sergeant Peterson was trying to calm her down, but Carmine kept screaming until the driver and passenger of the Mercedes Benz got out on the driver's side. She then went silent and stared.

It was her ex-husband, Kipfer Rightful, and his new bride. Carmine had heard Kipfer was back in town and newly remarried. She continued to stare. She then saw the new bride had a cat that looked exactly like her Rinny, except it was alive and not stuffed. The new bride was attractive, very attractive.

Kipfer, his new wife and the Rinny look-alike were walking towards her.

"Hello Carmine. I suppose it's not an unusual way to meet you again. You've put on some weight since the last time I saw you, but maybe it's just the dress. Carmine, this is my wife Carmi and her cat Spicey. You shouldn't have run that red light."

Carmine was silent for one of the first times in her life and continued to stare at Kipfer, Carmi and Spicey.

"Hi Carmine, it's a pleasure to meet you, but I guess not under these circumstances." Carmi put her hand out to shake hands with Carmine, but Carmine still didn't move.

"Carmine I need to see your driver's license," Sergeant Peterson said.

He repeated his request three times before Carmine went back to her Honda minivan to get her purse.

There were now 10 to 15 people standing around the accident. Ten of them volunteered to Sergeant Peterson to be witnesses to the accident.

Carmine made one last attempt to blame Kipfer for running the red light, but she was overwhelmed by the negative response she received from Sergeant Peterson, the volunteer witnesses, Kipfer and his new wife. The only one who didn't turn on her was the cat, Spicey. Carmine knew she'd always had a way with cats.

Patnude just stood on the corner of Cedar and Broad Street watching. He was pretty sure this was the first, and most likely the only time he would ever see Carmine at a loss for words.

A Surprise Meeting with Carmine Rightful

It was three days after Carmine ran into her ex and his new wife on Broad Street and Cedar when she stormed through Best Funeral Home's back door. She saw Patnude sitting behind his desk.

"Where's I.M.?" she shouted.

"He's out on an appointment. May I help you, Carmine?" Patnude replied.

Carmine looked around. She was still wearing her bright red tent dress, and her black and white Converse athletic shoes. Her bright red lipstick was more smeared than usual. She had a wild look in her eyes.

"Please sit down, Carmine. Would you like something to drink? Water or coffee?"

"Is the coffee fresh? If not, I'll take some bottles of your Costco water."

Patnude handed her two bottles of Costco water with the one on her right open.

"What can I do for you?" Patnude asked.

"Well, I wish I.M. were here. I prefer to talk with the in-charge person. I have found out, in the most difficult way, that if I don't talk to the head man I make little progress in resolving issues and problems. It was my mother who taught me this policy. Always deal with the top man or woman, or what or whomever calls the shots. Well, I now have a big, big problem. I closed my convenience store early to meet with I.M., but he is not here and now I have to meet with you, just my luck. Oh well, at least it's a start."

"What is your problem, Carmine? It's not the size of your coffin again, is it?"

"No. No. No. I'm fine with the 44-inch-wide model I selected. I will look petite in the 44-inch model, although I might change the color of the lining since I'm thinking of changing the color of my dress and I want them to blend and not clash, but maybe clashing colors will make me look more petite. I'm still thinking about it, but that should be an easy change. No, that's not my problem today, maybe tomorrow, but not today."

"What is your problem today?" Patnude asked.

"My ex-husband, Kipfer, is back in town with his slutty new wife, who looks like she's anorexic. I met them a few days ago. She even has a cat just like Rinny, but it isn't stuffed like my Rinny."

Carmine then pulled Rinny out of her bag by her tail. Patnude noticed Rinny's left glass eye was back in place, but it didn't match the color of Rinny's right eye. "I bet they bought that cat on purpose to upset me. But it doesn't matter since I have my Rinny whom I still love very much. Don't I, Rinny?"

As Carmine hugged Rinny, her new left glass eye popped out onto the floor and rolled under Patnude's desk.

Patnude had a non-visual mortician smile when he heard Rinny's glass eye hit the hard floor and roll.

"Would you get Rinny's eye? It keeps falling out. I actually have several replacements. I suppose I should have it re-glued. If I got down on the floor on my hands and knees I don't know if I could get up without your help. It sounded like it rolled into the corner. Do you have a flashlight?"

"I'll find Rinny's left eye," Patnude said as he got down on his hands and knees.

"Here it is. I found it. Would you like some scotch tape to hold it in?"

"No, I'll just pop it back in later. The tape would pull Rinny's fur out and it has stopped growing once I had her stuffed."

Patnude nodded as he looked at his watch; it was only 2:15 p.m.

"What is your problem with Kipfer being back in town and how may we help?"

"I heard that Kipfer now has ten convenience stores with gas pumps around the state. When we got divorced we only had two and I got the best one here in Globe, but it hasn't been doing so well lately. Nothing like it was doing when we were married. I didn't realize the stores were open 24 hours a day. That is just too much work for me. I open it at 10:00 in the morning and close it at 4:00 in the afternoon. I've also put on a few pounds since I've been running the store. I just nibble on whatever I can find when the store is open."

"I thought convenience stores with gas pumps were open 24 hours a day by definition."

"Well, not mine. Ten to four on weekdays and I'm closed on weekends, although I have been thinking about opening it on Saturdays, but I don't know if I'm up to it, if you know what I mean?"

"Anyway, what is your problem with Kipfer being back in town with his new wife?"

"She looks slutty to me and probably a money grabber. Kipfer is not very smart in dealing with women."

Patnude thought to himself, well maybe Kipfer has gotten smarter in dealing with women.

"I've heard she has a PhD and that she's a professor at the U of A, and comes from a wealthy family from Charleston, South Carolina."

"Oh, still looks slutty to me. I'm concerned for Kipfer since I told you that he is not too bright about women."

"Carmine, what is the problem you want us to help you with?"

"Oh—my problem! I almost forgot since you started jabbering and going on and on. I'm concerned about Kipfer having the burial plot next to me and my parents. I don't want to spend eternity with Kipfer lying right next to me. How do I get rid of him?"

Patnude pulled up the website for Forever Restful Cemetery and looked at the ownership of the burial plots.

"Kipfer has four burial plots to the right of you. It looks like he purchased the additional three plots a few days ago. Your options are to buy the burial plots from Kipfer or buy the plot to the left of your mother's plot. Oh, wait, you can't, since all of those plots are occupied."

Carmine slumped in her chair and pulled out her one-eyed Rinny with her left eye now missing out of its bag and hugged her tightly. Patnude thought Derwood Sloan, the taxidermist, must have used better glue on Rinny's right eye.

"I bet Kipfer is planning to get money from our auto accident to pay for those three plots. He always was a conniving bastard."

Patnude then heard Rinny's right eye pop out, hit the floor and roll under his desk. Carmine must have squeezed Rinny a little too hard. Rinny was now missing both eyes.

Another Surprise Visit from Carmine Rightful

I.M. was meeting with Kipfer and Carmi in his office. As was his policy, he always closed his office door when he was doing future funeral planning. Patnude was in his office with his door open. It was a little after 1:00 on a Thursday afternoon when he heard some commotion in the office reception area.

Carmine was arguing with Maria that she wanted to see I.M. now. She didn't care if he was in a meeting. She closed early so she could meet with him today. She didn't need an appointment to meet with I.M. She could meet with I.M. whenever it was convenient for her. Carmine was getting nowhere with Maria.

"I suggest you leave now and call and make an appointment with I.M. He can't see you now, end of discussion. Now, please leave," Maria demanded.

Carmine's face was now as red as her red tent dress, red hair and smeared red lipstick.

"Hello, Carmine. What seems to be the problem? May I help?" offered Patnude.

"I want to see I.M. You are no help. I want to move Kipfer's gravesite. I do not want to be lying beside him for eternity. Do you understand me? Are you listening to me?"

Just then I.M. emerged from his office, followed by Kipfer and Carmi, who was holding Spicey.

Carmine screamed, "I don't want to spend eternity lying alongside of him," pointing at Kipfer. "What can you do about it?" she shouted, as she nervously pulled Rinny, tail first from her bag.

Patnude noticed Rinny's eyes were now held in place by a long piece of scotch tape wrapped around her head.

Spicey was being held tightly by Carmi as it hissed at Rinny.

"You need to discuss your situation with Kipfer or select another gravesite."

"I don't want another gravesite," Carmine screamed as she attempted to run out of Best Funeral Home's office. She attempted to stuff Rinny back into her traveling bag as she got into her red Honda Minivan.

Unfortunately, Rinny missed the bag and was now resting on the parking lot's pavement. Unknowingly, Carmine backed over Rinny, and then got her again when she pulled forward and exited the parking lot.

Patnude ran out to pick up the crushed Rinny and was waving and yelling at Carmine as she sped away. Rinny now had two large tire tracks across her squished body.

Patnude couldn't help but notice that both of Rinny's eyes were still in place. The scotch tape had done the trick of securing her eyes.

Agree to Disagree

Almost two weeks had gone by since Sissie brought up the idea of buying the old building where Patnude was raised by his grandparents in Miami. It wasn't like her to drop something once she'd made up her mind. Especially something big like this. Not like Sissie at all.

It was early Wednesday afternoon, and Patnude had just finished buying office supplies under Maria's instructions. He pulled around back of Best Funeral Home and saw Sissie's car parked in the lot.

I.M.'s office door was closed, which indicated he was in a meeting, but Patnude didn't remember that he had any scheduled.

"Here are your office supplies."

"Who is I.M. meeting with?" Patnude asked Maria.

"You don't know?"

"No, I don't know."

"I.M.'s meeting with Sissie."

"My Sissie?"

"Weren't you listening? I.M.'s meeting with your Sissie. You didn't buy any blue pens for I.M., did you?"

Patnude shook his head no and answered, "Only the supplies you ordered."

Patnude pushed the four blue pens he bought for I.M. lower into his jacket pocket. He wondered why Sissie was meeting with I.M. Neither one of them said anything to him about a meeting. Patnude felt uncomfortable being out of the loop. He was still standing and looking at I.M.'s closed office door when it opened and Sissie and I.M. walked out.

"Okay, I think I got it. I will stand as far away as I can to study Rolfer's paintings. I'm still going to concentrate on the orange one, it's my favorite. Oh, hi, Patnude. You know Sissie don't you?"

Sissie was dressed as the professional Sissie. Patnude knew that she and I.M.

had to be conducting business.

"Hi Patnude. Would you like to buy me lunch?"

Sissie kissed Patnude on the cheek. She pushed her glasses back up as they slid down her nose. This was her intellectual look.

Patnude was silent. He didn't know why.

"Patnude, it was a yes or no question. Would you like to buy me lunch?"

"Hmmm, yes, I think so."

"Well that's the positive answer I was looking for. Let's go, you can drive. See you later on Friday, I.M."

Patnude slipped the contraband blue pens to I.M. when Maria turned her head away. I.M. just nodded yes and smiled.

Patnude and Sissie went to the Copper Nugget for lunch. After ordering, Patnude could no longer control his curiosity.

"What were you and I.M. meeting about?" he asked.

"Aren't you the nosey one? We were meeting about The Complete Hardware & Variety Store. I.M. wants to rent a significant portion of the first floor and wants me to do the design for the Miami Best Funeral Home."

"Are we buying the building?"

"I don't know if we are buying it, but *I'm* certainly buying it. I told you that a while ago. You haven't sounded very keen on the idea and seem to avoid the topic every time I bring it up."

Patnude didn't know why, but he felt hesitant about buying Pa and Ma's old building with Sissie.

"I think we need to talk about it. I'm not sure that I'm ready to buy it."

"Okay, then don't. I will buy it and you can stay with me."

"Can you afford to buy it and make the necessary repairs?"

"Yes—with I.M. renting most of the first floor, I'll be fine. What are you afraid of? Buying real estate with me, or moving back to your old homestead? I'll even give you your old room back. I bet it's the long-term commitment with me, isn't it?"

"No, I don't think so. I don't know. I'm just not ready, at least not right now."

Sissie looked at Patnude and just shook her head. "Eat your lunch as I have a 2:00 appointment this afternoon."

It was a quiet ride back to Best Funeral Home. As Sissie opened the car door to leave, she said, "Am I going to see you tonight?"

"I don't know. I have things that I need to do."

"Like what kind of things?"

"Just some things, that's all."

"Goodbye, Patnude. Call me when you've taken care of all of your things."

Patnude was depressed as he walked into Best Funeral Home. Maria was waiting for him by the door holding up four blue pens.

"Did you buy these blue pens for I.M.? Well, did you?"

Patnude didn't answer as he walked into his office, closed the door and sat down behind his desk. He was depressed and came to the realization that he couldn't deal with women, at least two women. He secretly wished for several deaths, no one in particular, but just some, so he could be busy at Best Funeral Home and take his mind off of Sissie and Maria.

Carmine Rightful, Yet Again

It was exactly three weeks later on a Thursday afternoon that Patnude heard Carmine talking with Maria. But this time—she was polite and sane.

"Patnude, do you have a few minutes to talk with Carmine?" Maria asked.

You mean listen to Carmine, Patnude thought to himself.

"I do, please come into my office. Would you like some water?"

"Yes, please, but just one bottle."

Patnude couldn't help but notice that Carmine was holding a live cat that looked like the crushed Rinny, who was now lying or resting on top of his credenza in the corner of his office.

"Did you get a new cat?" Patnude asked.

"Yes, I have. His name is Spicey and he is just adorable and I love him so much. He was a gift from Carmi. She is just an angel. She is becoming one of my best friends. I don't why you were so against her and thought she was a slut and money grabber when she married Kipfer. They really make a perfect couple. They were made for each other. Mother and I are having them over for dinner tonight. Mother just loves Carmi and she is thrilled with Spicey. I'm also thinking of having you apologize to Carmi for the things you said about her. But probably not since that is confidential talk, just between you and me. But again, you were totally wrong. She is just an angel. I love her. Do you have a little dish where I can give Spicey some water? I think he is thirsty."

Patnude got a small dish and of course had to use Costco bottled water since Spicey does not drink Globe tap water. *No siree*, Patnude thought.

Patnude was stunned. He could hardly speak, he couldn't help notice that Carmine was not wearing her red tent dress, her hair was a more mellow red, her lipstick was not smeared and a more subdued red and she was wearing leather sandals instead of her black and white Converse athletic shoes.

"Do you like my new beige dress? Carmi picked it out and thought it made me look more petite. I have actually started my diet and maybe won't need a 44-inch-wide coffin after all, but we will see."

"Tell me again what happened?" Patnude asked.

"After I left here last week in sort of a huff, Kipfer, Carmi and Spicey followed me to my convenience store. We talked for a long time since I didn't have any customers. Carmi suggested that she and Kipfer exchange gravesites, that way I would be lying alongside Carmi and we would spend eternity telling stories about Kipfer. Kipfer agreed, but he didn't really have any choice since Carmi said that's what they were going to do. Then she said that Spicey really loves me and that he belongs with me, and then she gave him to me. Can you imagine that?"

Patnude shook his head no.

"And Kipfer, God bless him, said my store looked a mess and that he'd like to take over managing it and share the profits with me. It is now back to being open 24 hours a day and business has significantly improved since he took over running it. You should see what the store looks like now—just like it used to! Carmi took me shopping for new clothes and she demanded I get a full beauty treatment, which I did. She also signed me up for an exercise class. She is just an angel. Kipfer is so lucky he found her, and he knows it because I have told him a whole bunch of times. I just wanted to bring you up to date on what's happened in the last few weeks and thank you for all of your help. I appreciate it." Carmine then hugged Patnude. "Thanks again for everything."

Patnude pointed towards the credenza in the corner with the mangled Rinny lying on top. "Oh that, you can keep her, Spicey doesn't want her around our house."

Spicey hissed as he noticed Rinny lying on top of the credenza in the corner.

As Carmine left Best Funeral Home's office, Patnude slowly and silently slipped Rinny into the wastebasket next to his desk. He thought he heard one of Rinny's glass eyes fall out, but he didn't bother to look.

A Drowning Provides an Opportunity

Patnude was sitting in his office after lunch at the Copper Nugget. He was depressed since he missed Sissie and didn't know what to do. For some reason he was afraid; no, not afraid, maybe uneasy about going back to The Complete Hardware & Variety Store building where he grew up. He knew he'd disappointed Sissie when he indirectly refused to buy it with her and then kind of broke up with her. He hadn't come out and said the words, but he'd stopped all contact, unless they crossed paths at the Copper Nugget, in which case he'd be cordial and say hi and how are you. He was really being stupid and he didn't know why. It wasn't like him, or maybe it was. I.M. walked into Patnude's office.

"Why so glum? You look terrible. Cheer up we have a new death."

"Who?"

"One of the Mullin twins from Miami, you must have known them."

"I do, Mahoney and Maroon. It must have been Mahoney since I heard he was going to fly his flying lawn chair from Globe to Safford. I guess it would be some kind of Arizona record. What happened to Mahoney?"

"Nothing happened to Mahoney. His lawn chair landed safely in the shallow water of San Carlos Lake."

"It was Maroon who died."

"Yes, he drowned in San Carlos Lake in the deep water by Coolidge Dam."

"What happened?"

"Well, Mahoney was making great progress following U.S. 70 on his way to Safford, when a strong easterly wind blew him towards San Carlos Lake. Maroon followed him in their father's old 1972 Ford pickup. On their way to the lake, two hawks tried to land on the helium balloons that were holding Mahoney up. The balloons exploded from the hawks' claws. The explosion scared the one hawk away, but the other one was more determined. It must have been a female."

Patnude nodded in agreement.

"This hawk, again most likely a female, continued to try and land on a balloon, which continued to explode and scare her away for a minute before she would try again. As you would expect, Mahoney was jettisoning everything he could. The last thing to go was what was left of his 12 pack of beer. Mahoney continued to drop lower and lower. He also got closer to San Carlos Lake and then over the lake. Maroon must have panicked since neither one of them could swim, and the hawk kept popping the balloons. When it looked like Mahoney was about to splash into the lake, Maroon must have quit paying attention to his driving and drove off the embankment close to Coolidge Dam where the water is the deepest. He didn't get out of the pickup even though the windows were open. He drowned inside the cab as it filled with water."

"What about Mahoney?"

"He had a soft landing in about 4 feet of water and just walked out. The alleged female hawk kept trying to land on the helium filled balloons until they all exploded. Mahoney didn't know what happened to Maroon and it wasn't until later that the sunken 1972 Ford pickup was discovered from the floating debris."

"How sad—the Mullin brothers were always very close and did everything together. Mahoney must be pretty broken up."

"I heard he is, and he gave a statement to the paper that he has taken his last lawn chair flight."

"Where is Maroon's body?"

"The San Carlos Indian Reservation Hospital. I'll ride with you. I think Maria is coming in today for month-end. I'm pretty sure I have hidden all my blue pens, but you never know. She's a pretty good detective."

As usual, Patnude was driving the new used Buick hearse.

"Were you a close friend of the Mullin brothers?"

"No, not really, I just knew them since Miami is a small town."

"I'm not sure how they made a living. They've lived in their parents' old house all these years, even though both parents are deceased. I once heard their father received a large inheritance. I think they just hung around Miami, drank beer and Mahoney did the flying lawn chair gig from time to time. I don't remember them doing much dating. I would see them once in a while and just say hi and so forth. Mahoney is going to be devastated. Their entire lives were spent together. I believe they only had one car, their father's old 1972 Ford pickup that Maroon drove into San Carlos Lake. I don't know how Mahoney is going to cope with Maroon's death. I guess he is going to have to buy another car, or most likely another pickup."

Patnude and I.M. picked up Maroon's body from the San Carlos Reservation Hospital and were driving back to Globe.

"His forehead is all bruised. He must have been knocked out when he hit the water, which is why he didn't leave the Ford pickup," I.M. said.

"Open casket?"

"I think so."

"What's happening with you and Sissie?"

"I think we kind of broke up."

"Let me give you some fatherly advice—un-breakup. You are losing a very special person. She is truly one in a million and you ain't. You need to call her."

"I know."

"Have you seen the status of the buildout of our Miami funeral parlor? It is looking prestigious. Sissie did a fabulous design. It should be completed in two weeks."

Mahoney Mullin was waiting for the arrival of his dead brother. Patnude backed the hearse into the garage and went over and hugged Mahoney.

"Do you think Maroon suffered?" Mahoney asked.

"We don't think so. He wasn't wearing his seat belt and we think he was knocked out from the impact of the truck hitting the water."

"Thanks, Patnude. I've decided, out of respect for Maroon, to give up lawn chair flying. However, I've been contacted by an agent who wants me to write a book about Maroon and me, and my lawn chair flights. If you find Maroon's cell phone amongst his personal belongings from the hospital, will you let me know? He took pictures of my last flight, and I'm hoping one of them will make a great book cover. The agent thinks I have good potential for TV or a movie, maybe both. What do you think of *My Last Flight* as a title?"

"It sounds interesting."

"Let me know if you find Maroon's phone and I will see you at the funeral."

Patnude acknowledged to himself how quickly Mahoney seemed to have gotten over the death of his twin brother. So much for the closeness of twin brothers?

Maroon Mullin's Funeral

Maroon Mullin's viewing was scheduled for Wednesday afternoon and the burial late Thursday morning. Since the buildout was incomplete for Best Funeral Home's new Miami funeral parlor, the viewing and service was held in their Globe facility.

Maroon's casket was open since I.M. and Patnude were able to cover up all of the bruises on his forehead. Patnude was present for the entire three-hour viewing since he knew many of the mourners from Miami.

Maroon's twin brother Mahoney was also present for the entire three-hour viewing time. He took many photos of Maroon in his casket and the attending mourners.

Mahoney was pleased and repeatedly thanked Patnude for giving him Maroon's personal items, including his cell phone. He commented to Patnude that being submerged in San Carlos Lake didn't hurt the photos on Maroon's cell phone. He thought several of the photos would make a great book cover for his new book.

Patnude noticed that Mahoney drove up in a new, large Ford all-wheel drive pickup. It was red and white, which was the color of the helium balloons that Mahoney used to attach to his flying lawn chair.

Around 4:30, Clyde "Scoop" Cooper walked into Best Funeral Home and headed directly towards Mahoney. They shook hands and Scoop gave Mahoney a manly hug. Scoop looked the same as the last time Patnude saw him. He was short, overweight, balding with a comb over, large thick glasses with black plastic frames, bright green short-sleeved shirt with large yellow flowers, dark brown cargo shorts with bulging pockets and sandals with calf length black socks. Patnude noticed there were no holes in Scoop's black socks like there were the last time he saw Scoop.

Mahoney and Scoop moved over to the casket and stood looking at Maroon. They pointed at Maroon as they whispered to each other, and then Mahoney motioned at Patnude to join them.

"Hello Scoop, how are you?"

"Fine, good to see you again Patrick."

"My name is Patnude."

"Oh, that's right, Patnude as in, oh hell I don't know what Patnude is in. Anyway, it doesn't matter. Patnude, after the service, I would like to take several professional photos of Maroon. I will only need about 10 to 15 minutes, okay?"

"Yes, as long as it is okay with Mahoney."

"Scoop is doing a story about my brother and me for the Arizona News: about our relationship, my brother's death, and the end of my flying chair adventures, out of respect for him. I've also engaged Scoop to be my publicist for my new book, or who knows—*books*."

Just then, a short man dressed in black with slick black hair combed back over his head and wearing large dark sunglasses walked in. He smiled when he saw Mahoney and Scoop and walked directly over to them.

"Patnude, this is my agent for the book, or most likely the series of books, Falcon Fabian," Mahoney said.

"Please da meet ya," Falcon said with a heavy east coast accent as he gave Patnude a used car salesman handshake.

Mahoney, Scoop and Falcon were talking and smiling at each other while Scoop setup his camera. He proceeded to take numerous pictures of Mahoney standing by Maroon's coffin. After about 15 minutes, all three left Best Funeral Home.

Patnude no had no doubt that Mahoney was over his twin brother's death. Mahoney was exploiting the once in a lifetime opportunity that Maroon's death had provided to him.

Patnude then thought maybe Mahoney is doing exactly what Maroon would want him to do. Life can be confusing at times.

Rinny Is Resurrected

It was Thursday morning and Patnude was updating Carmine Rightful's current change to the color of the lining in her 44-inch-wide coffin. She wanted one side a mild pink and the other side a mild blue, which was Carmine's description of the coffin liner colors. She planned on wearing a pink and blue dress for her funeral.

Maria, the part-time bookkeeper walked in carrying a cat. It was black, tan and white, and was not moving. Not moving at all.

Patnude had a panic flashback. Was Maria's cat the resurrected Rinny, Carmine Rightful's abandoned and dumped stuffed cat from a few weeks ago?

"Maria, what is that?"

"It's a cat decoration for my office, just a little personal touch. My office was missing something like that," Maria said.

"Is that Carmine Rightful's old stuffed cat, Rinny, that I threw in the trash?"

"Yes, it is. I couldn't tolerate her being thrown in the trash. I found Derwood Sloan and he agreed to give Rinny a beauty treatment and clean her up. You can hardly even see the tire marks where Carmine ran over her twice. Plus, she has new eyes now, they are yellow and her tail has been refastened more securely. I just love her."

Patnude thought Maria sounded like Carmine before she got Spicey.

Maria cleaned off a bookshelf and placed Rinny in the center of it, overlooking her office as if she were in command, or on guard duty.

Patnude hoped that Derwood used better glue on Rinny's new eyes than he did originally.

Maria placed two cans of cat food behind Rinny and a rubber mouse that squeaked when you squeezed it, in front of her paws.

"What do you think?" Maria asked. "Doesn't Rinny look perfect, just like she is on duty protecting me? I just love her. What do you think? It feels more like my office now."

"Is there cat food in the cans?"

"No, I opened them on the bottom and took the cat food out. But don't they give a realistic touch?"

I.M. walked in, looked up and saw Rinny and then asked, "What's that cat doing in our office?"

A Late Friday Night and
Canned Chicken Noodle Soup

atnude was putting the final touches on Agunzo Smith for his funeral service and his burial tomorrow. It was almost 6:30 on a Friday evening, and Agunzo's widow was late in dropping off clothes for his final dressing and appearance to friends and loved ones. Agunzo's widow's name was Apple. Patnude thought both Agunzo and Apple were unusual first names. Maybe that was what attracted them to each other. Their initials were the same, A.E.S., very unusual. Agunzo's middle name was Edward and Apple's was Edna. Patnude didn't know what kind of turnout to expect tomorrow, since Agunzo and Apple owned and operated AES Collection Services for many years in the Globe-Miami area.

Agunzo had been an aggressive bad debt collector and was not the most popular person with many local residents. He was threatened frequently whilst collecting delinquent accounts for his clients. Shot at numerous times, but never hit, except of course for the last time three days ago. It wasn't the gunshot wound that killed Agunzo, since it was just a 22-caliber bullet that went in and out of his right butt cheek. It was the repossessed freezer loaded with butchered and dressed wild game that fell off his 2-wheel hand truck on top of Agunzo and crushed him to death. It was Butcher Jim's wife Janey who shot Agunzo in the butt. Janey was arrested on a second-degree murder charge. Patnude knew for sure that Butcher Jim and Janey would not be at Agunzo's funeral service. Patnude had two thoughts as he finished with Agunzo. He wondered what happened to the frozen butchered game meat in Butcher Jim's freezer and if Agunzo would have bled to death from being shot in the butt with a .22. He then thought, *strange things to wonder about.*

I.M. walked in and asked, "Are you all finished preparing Agunzo?"

"Yes."

"Do you and Sissie want to come over for dinner tomorrow night?"

"Well, we are not actually dating now."

"I thought you were going to fix that."

"Well, I haven't fixed it yet."

"Can you do it by tomorrow night or should I just ask each of you as an individual for dinner tomorrow night?"

Patnude looked at I.M., nonplussed.

"Okay, I won't ask either one of you. Dinner for tomorrow night is now cancelled."

"Did you ever use Agunzo to collect delinquent accounts?"

"A couple of times, he always collected. I think most people paid from embarrassment. I don't remember her name, but one widow wanted to return her husband's ashes if we wrote off our accounts receivable. She wanted to keep the urn for some unknown reason and put his ashes in an old Mason jar for us to keep."

"You didn't accept his ashes, did you?"

"Of course not. If I remember right, this was an account Agunzo collected for us. I bet there are quite a few people in Globe-Miami who will be pleased to hear Agunzo is dead."

Patnude didn't feel up to making dinner tonight or going to his empty apartment. He decided to go to his favorite restaurant, Le Citron. When he pulled into the parking lot, he saw two orange Mini Coopers parked next to each other. The license plate on the first Mini was ITSHRNK and the other was ITSHRNK2.

Patnude thought, *oh no, Sissie and Famine are having dinner at Le Citron.* He didn't know what to do since he wanted to see Sissie, but didn't know what to say. It would certainly be more difficult with Famine there. He looked up and, oh no, they were walking out of the restaurant. They stopped, waved and walked over.

"Hi, Patnude, what are you doing sitting in the parking lot?" Famine asked.

"I, ah, I just pulled up and finished a call."

"Oh, your car's not running."

"I shut it off. Hi Sissie, how are you?"

"I'm fine, Patnude. When you're brave enough, give me a call and I'll give you a tour of your old homestead. Take care. See you later."

Sissie got into ITSHRNK2 and Famine got into ITSHRNK and the two orange Mini Coopers left Le Citron's parking lot.

Patnude had lost his appetite. He left the Le Citron parking lot and went home. He heated up a can of chicken noodle soup for dinner and he felt like kicking himself in the ass for being such a—whatever.

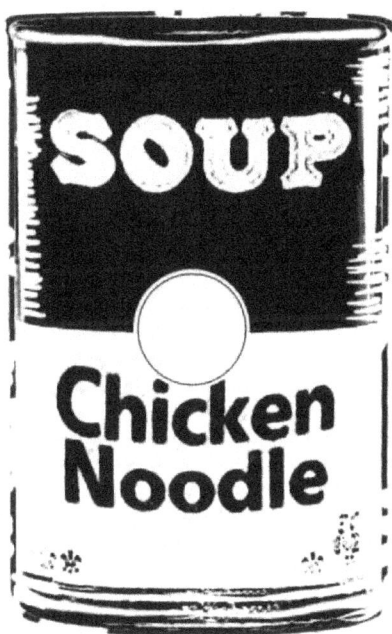

Agunzo Smith's Funeral
and Afterwards

The Saturday funeral service for Agunzo Smith was dignified. Only a few people poked his body with their fingers to make sure Agunzo was dead. They smiled when he didn't move. All of the flowers were from a few relatives and the business people that used his collection services.

Apple spent most of the viewing time standing alongside Agunzo's coffin, looking down at him and touching his hand.

"Agunzo was really a very sensitive man. He always put on an act when he collected delinquent accounts. He never enjoyed repossessions. His macho, I-don't-care attitude was just an act. It's terrible that he died doing his job. He was killed by a deadbeat who didn't honor his obligations. I always warned him to be careful on repossessions. I will miss Agunzo. I will miss him very much," Apple said as she received a hug from Patnude.

Patnude was surprised to see Butcher Jim at the viewing. He walked up to Apple, looking at her for a few seconds or more.

"Apple, I'm sorry about what happened to Agunzo. It was all my fault for not making my monthly payments, and then things just got out of hand when he repossessed the freezer. I don't know why Janey grabbed the gun and shot him. I pulled the freezer off of him as soon as I could, but it was too late since—he was already dead. I'm sorry for everything. It was all my fault."

Apple didn't respond except for nodding her head. Butcher Jim went over to the corner of the viewing room and sat down. He had tears rolling down his cheeks as he stared at Agunzo in his coffin.

Patnude thought Butcher Jim was correct. It was his fault, and he could have done something to prevent Agunzo's death and his wife Janey's potential punishment.

Patnude realized he needed to do something.

After Agunzo's burial service at Forever Restful Cemetery, and after Patnude returned the hearse to the garage, he walked over to his favorite coffee shop, which happened to be Sissie's favorite as well.

He opened the coffee shop door and saw Sissie from behind, reading a book. He ordered an iced coffee and walked over to her table.

"May I join you?" he asked.

Sissie looked up, smiled and answered, "Sure, no other tables empty?"

"There are some, but I like this one."

"Oh, please sit down then."

"You are always a knockout when you wear that dress. That's the dress you were wearing when we first had coffee together."

Sissie looked at Patnude with a wily smile.

Sissie was wearing her blue sleeveless dress, short and low cut. It was one of her T and A dresses.

Patnude's iced coffee was served.

"Are you available for dinner tonight? I'll buy, no dutch treat."

Sissie put her book down, took a sip of her coffee and looked at Patnude.

"Let me check my calendar and see if I am free."

After about sixty seconds Sissie looked up from her cell phone calendar, "Looks like I'm available tonight. Pick me up at 6:30. You know where I live. Park in back and come upstairs, if you're not afraid. I have to go. See you at 6:30."

Sissie left the coffee shop and, as usual when she wore that blue dress, all males in the coffee shop watched her—including Patnude.

Patnude smiled and felt pleased with himself for the first time in a while.

Sissie Learns How to Make Patnude Act Smarter

Patnude arrived at exactly 6:30 at the back of the old hardware store building which was now Best Funeral Home's Miami funeral parlor. Sissie's office was also located on the first floor, with her residence on the second floor.

Patnude was nervous about having dinner with Sissie and being back at the old building. He had to admit it looked pretty good though. Sissie did a great job on its rehab.

He was still wearing his grey funeral parlor suit since he didn't get a chance to go home and change into more casual attire. He wondered what Sissie would be wearing. Maybe the blue T and A dress she had on earlier, most likely not. He looked up and saw Sissie standing queenly at the top of the stairs. She walked slowly down the stairs—very slowly.

Sissie was wearing a soft blue dress with short sleeves that buttoned down the front and stopped at her knees. The first couple of buttons from the collar downward were unbuttoned. Her shoes were highly polished beige ballet flats. Her appearance was regal.

Patnude got out of his white 4-door Chevrolet Impala and reached the bottom of the stairs at the same time as Sissie.

"Hi, you look very noble and stately tonight," Patnude said as he gave Sissie a soft hug. Sissie did not reciprocate.

"You look very funeral parlor-ish."

"Sorry, I didn't get a chance to change. I thought you were going to give me a tour of your new abode and my old abode."

"I don't think you're ready for a tour just yet. Maybe later, we'll see," Sissie said as she opened the car door, slid in and gently closed the door.

"Is Le Citron okay?" Patnude asked.

"Yes."

It was a quiet ride to Le Citron with just a little chit-chat. Mary Ellen, the hostess, greeted them and brought them to their favorite table. Patnude ordered a bottle of Sissie's favorite wine, Chateau Ste. Michelle Chardonnay.

After the wine was poured, Patnude made a toast, "To us." Sissie only clinked her glass once, not her usual two or three times.

"Why did you ask me out to dinner tonight?" Sissie asked.

"Because I missed being with you and realized that I was being foolish, acting immature and decided I needed to correct the situation that I caused."

"What made you realize what you just said?"

"I realized it the minute I started acting like a jerk, but then I didn't know what to do about it, so I did nothing and felt miserable not being with you. Today I realized since I caused the situation between us, that I was the only one who could correct it and I needed to do something immediately. Which is what I did as soon as Agunzo Smith's funeral service was over. I guessed you might be at the coffee shop and you were. I apologize for being such a jerk and I will do everything in my power not to ever let it happen again. If it does, you need to take me off to the side and keep dope slapping me until I realize I'm being stupid again."

Patnude felt a sharp pain to his left cheek and heard a loud whack when Sissie slapped once and then again. Patnude started to rub his left cheek.

"Slaps like that?" Sissie asked.

"Yes, that hurt. You may have cut the inside of my cheek."

Patnude again felt and heard another loud whack to his left cheek followed by yet another hard slap from Sissie.

"Are you starting to feel wiser now?" Sissie asked.

Patnude continued to rub his left cheek as he answered, "Yes, I most definitely am feeling really, really smart now. I don't know if I could ever feel any smarter."

"Good," Sissie said, as she picked up her wine glass to make a toast. "Here's to us," and she clinked her wine glass three times with Patnude.

He smiled as he continued to rub his left cheek and reached for Sissie's right hand to hold.

Sissie smiled as she said, "You think you are so clever," as she slapped his right cheek with her left hand.

"I do think you are looking a little smarter now, the slaps must be working."

Fellow restaurant patrons couldn't help but hear the slaps, which forced them to watch Patnude and Sissie. Patnude sort of smiled as he looked at them and continued to rub his cheeks.

"Let's order, I'm hungry. Maybe you should only have something soft, like soup or mashed potatoes. Thanks for the tip on how to make you act smarter. I'll remember it for future use."

Patnude was pleased to hear the words, "future use."

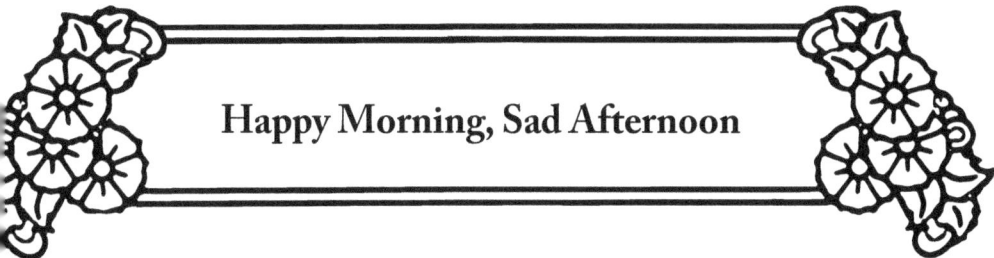

Happy Morning, Sad Afternoon

Sissie agreed to spend the night with Patnude at his apartment. The following morning, after breakfast, Patnude drove Sissie back to Miami. They both were pleased with themselves and their feelings for each other. Sissie was wearing shorts and one of Patnude's long-sleeved shirts and her polished beige ballet flats. Her soft blue dress was neatly folded on her lap. Sissie looked over at Patnude and spoke, "Assuming last night wasn't a one-night stand on your part, what are your thoughts or desires about tonight?"

"I would like to repeat our one-night stand tonight. What if I came over to your new—I'm not sure what you call it?"

"How about Patnude's childhood home, remodeled? No, I don't think you are ready to visit your remodeled childhood home yet. We need more time together before that happens. How about if I stop by your apartment at about 6:30 and you can make dinner?"

"Okay, you want me to make dinner tonight?"

"You have a choice, I will make dinner or I will make fantastic love with you, but I won't do both. You don't have to decide right now. Let me know your choice sometime today, okay?"

"Let me think about it, but I'm leaning towards making dinner tonight."

"Good choice. Maybe giving you dope slaps is working after all, time will tell."

Patnude pulled in back of his old childhood home and Sissie's new home. He jumped out quickly to open Sissie's door. After getting out, she put her arms around his neck and gave him a gentle, passionate kiss.

"Until tonight at 6:30, don't forget to let me know if you want me to make dinner tonight."

"I'm still thinking about it."

Sissie surprised Patnude with another dope slap to his right cheek but a little more gently than last night's slaps.

"I've made a decision—I'll cook dinner tonight."

Sissie looked at her right hand as she started to climb her stairs and then looked at Patnude and said, "The dope slaps seem to be working."

For a second or two, Patnude wondered if giving Sissie the dope slap option was a good idea. But he concluded it had brought them back together. Who knows, maybe it would help him be smarter in his forever relationship with her. However, his cheek still hurt a little.

Patnude walked into Best Funeral Home still smiling. He was happy that he and Sissie were back together.

"Good morning. You look happy today," I.M. said.

"I am. I followed your advice—and Sissie and I are back together."

"You never should have broken up. Don't let it happen again. You have someone waiting to see you."

"Who?"

"Butcher Jim."

"What does he want?"

"He wouldn't say, he wants to meet with you."

Patnude walked into the reception area and greeted Butcher Jim, and then led him to the conference room.

"Butcher Jim, how can I help you?"

"I think I need your help. You were standing next to Apple Smith when I talked to her at Agunzo's wake. I feel responsible for his death. If I would have just made my monthly payments, Agunzo would still be alive and my wife Janey would not be facing second-degree murder charges. Although, we think we might be able to get her charges lowered."

"How can I help?" Patnude was confused about where this conversation was going.

"I would like to volunteer my services to help Apple with her difficult collections and repossessions, at no charge of course. That way maybe I could help her keep AES Collection Services open. I owe her that much at a minimum. I think my image in town would help with the collection or even repossessions of her most serious delinquent accounts. It is the least I can do. Would you talk to her for me, please?"

"How long would you be able to provide your services?"

"For a while, I don't know how long. I guess as long as I was needed to help her. Agunzo's death was directly my fault. It just shows you what can go wrong when you screw up."

"Okay, I will talk with Apple and get back with you. I'm impressed with your acceptance of responsibility for your actions."

"I knew Agunzo and he was a good guy. He should not have died from being crushed by a freezer full of butchered game meat."

"Oh, I do have a question. What happened to the freezer with the butchered game meat in it?"

"After the ambulance took Agunzo's body to the hospital, I wheeled the freezer back into my butcher shop and plugged it in. It's there now, and full of the butchered game meat. I have finally started making my delinquent monthly payments, for all it's worth."

As Butcher Jim was leaving Best Funeral Home, an ambulance and two police cars sped by with their sirens blaring.

Butcher Jim thought they were heading to his part of town.

Later in the afternoon, Patnude was planning dinner for him and Sissie when I.M. walked into his office and sat down.

"You look serious, what's wrong?"

"I just heard that Butcher Jim's wife, Janey, committed suicide this morning in their butcher shop. A customer found her lying on the floor behind a meat cooler. She slit her wrists. Butcher Jim found out about her suicide when he returned to his shop after his meeting with you. The police and paramedics were there when he arrived. She had been dead for several hours."

"How terrible. Poor Butcher Jim must be devastated."

"He called a few minutes ago and wants us to do her funeral. He'll be in tomorrow morning to meet with you to plan it."

Patnude felt sad and knew the evening ahead with Sissie would now have a somber tint to it. He thought, as he frequently does, about how the life of a mortician is filled with sadness, on some days more than others, and he couldn't help but wonder what Butcher Jim was going through.

Another Night with Sissie and More Bad News

At breakfast the following morning, Patnude was more quiet than usual as he and Sissie were having breakfast.

"I like having breakfast with you," said Sissie.

"You've told me that before, but I don't know why since I eat in silence and read the newspaper. Thank you for being with me last night. Sorry for the no sex thing, but I just wasn't... I guess I just wasn't."

Sissie got up and kissed Patnude on the cheek. "I liked being with you last night. I'll be back tonight and the rules still apply."

"What rules?"

"If you make dinner then maybe we will have a romantic evening. Did you forget?" Sissie then gave Patnude a semi-gentle dope slap.

"Oh, now I remember."

"The dope slaps are working. I'll see you tonight," and then Sissie left for her first meeting.

Patnude smiled and realized how much he liked being with Sissie. How could he have been so dumb before?

Butcher Jim was waiting in the reception area at Best Funeral Home when Patnude arrived. Butcher Jim looked sad, solemn and tired.

"Good morning, Butcher Jim. How are you holding up? I'm so sorry about Janey—what a tragedy."

Butcher Jim mumbled a "good morning" and followed Patnude into this office.

"I want a modest and semi-private funeral for Janey. I want her cremated and I plan to keep her ashes in an urn for a while before I spread them out, somewhere, but right now I'm not sure where."

"Again, I'm so sorry about Janey. She will be missed by all who knew her."

"I still can't believe Janey committed suicide. She and our attorney were so positive that the charges against her would be reduced since she only shot Agunzo in the butt with a .22 caliber. She said it was his fault the freezer fell off the 2-wheel hand truck and crushed him. He didn't load it correctly, he didn't strap it to the hand truck, and he should have had help. Plus, it was filled with our game meat that was more valuable than the freezer. She was mad and considered Agunzo a thief, stealing our inventory. I have no idea what changed and caused her to commit suicide. It just doesn't make sense to me that Janey committed suicide by slitting her wrists. It's not something she would do. She was always a survivor and fighter. I just don't get it."

"Where is Janey's body?" Patnude asked.

"At the hospital, the police wanted to do an autopsy, but with both of her wrists slit I don't believe it is necessary."

"Do you have a security camera at your butcher shop?"

"Yes."

"Have you reviewed the video recording? Did you tell the police about the camera?"

"No, I forgot about it since it is sort of hidden and the shock of Janey's death."

"You need to do both now. I will draw up the funeral contract and you can come back this afternoon to review and sign it. Now go and tell the police about your security camera."

"Oh, Butcher Jim, what's your and Janey's last name? I don't believe I ever knew it."

"It's Butcher, that's why I'm a butcher and known as Butcher Jim."

Patnude smiled, shook his head and thought *only in Globe, Arizona.*

It was around closing time for Best Funeral Home and Butcher Jim had not returned to sign the funeral contract for his wife Janey. Patnude thought this was strange. It didn't seem like him at all. Patnude was putting on his grey suit jacket to leave for the day when I.M. walked in.

"Sit down, Patnude, I have shocking news for you, and most likely we will have another funeral," I.M. quietly stated.

"What do you mean? What are you talking about?"

"Well, Janey Butcher did not commit suicide. She was murdered."

"What! By who?"

"Apple Smith, who did commit suicide when the police arrived to arrest her at AES Collection Service's office. She shot herself in the head as the police entered her office."

"Oh, my God, what happened?"

"The security camera at the butcher shop shows Apple giving Janey something to drink and within a few minutes, she passes out and Apple then slits both of Janey's wrists, then leaves the butcher shop. She must have missed the security camera or didn't care and just wanted revenge for the death of Agunzo."

"How did you find out about this?"

"Sergeant Peterson told me a few minutes ago."

"How terrible, I wonder if Butcher Jim knows?"

Just then Butcher Jim walked into Patnude's office.

"I'm back to sign Janey's funeral contract papers. I assume you heard what happened. I'm in shock. Three deaths caused by me because I stopped making my monthly installment payments on my new freezer. Who would have ever thought this could happen here in Globe where everybody knows everybody? I can hardly believe that Apple killed Janey in cold blood. How cruel and deliberate. I assume you didn't talk with Apple regarding my offer to help her?"

"No, I called her yesterday and left a message for her to call me, but she never did."

"I wondered how Janey had slit both of her wrists when the police told me, but I guessed it was possible. Thank you for reminding me of having a security camera. If you hadn't, we all would have thought Janey committed suicide. I guess I can now say that Apple Smith was a bad apple, sort of funny in a sad way."

Butcher Jim signed the funeral contract for Janey and left.

"He is taking all of this better than I anticipated," Patnude said.

"I guess we will be busy next week with two funerals. Temper, revenge and fear can be good for the funeral business," I.M. stated.

"Sad but true," Patnude replied.

A Brave Patnude Returns
to His Old Home

Patnude and Sissie were having breakfast together on a Thursday morning. Patnude had already shined Sissie's shoes and selected her clothes for the day, and was therefore allowed to read the newspaper while he ate. Sissie required only a minimal response to her questions and comments.

"Patnude, I have been thinking…I believe you're ready for a tour of your old homestead on Saturday, maybe spend the night. Isn't Best Funeral Home having their first Miami funeral service on Saturday?"

"Yes, we are. Do you really think I'm ready for the tour?"

"I think so, there has been significant improvement in your smartness since the dope slap program commenced. I believe you are now ready for the tour."

Early Saturday evening, Patnude was climbing the back stairs to his old home where Ma and Pa raised him. He was carrying a bouquet of daisies and a bottle of wine; both were Sissie's favorites. He felt nervous and apprehensive and didn't know why. He hadn't been in his old home in years. In fact, since Ma and Pa died. He rang the bell and Sissie promptly opened the door.

"Well. Well. Who do we have here?" It isn't the brave Patnude is it, bringing gifts? Thank you, please come in."

Sissie hugged and kissed Patnude, grabbed the wine and flowers and said, "Follow me and then I will give you a tour."

Patnude followed her to the kitchen. Everything looked so different from how he remembered it, and it was.

Sissie opened the wine and poured two goblets of wine. "Here's to the brave Patnude and his old homestead tour." As usual, Sissie clinked their goblets three times. "Take another sip or drink, you might need it," Sissie instructed.

Patnude followed instructions since he did not want a Sissie dope slap.

"As you can see, I tore down a whole bunch of walls to create a large open living area. The kitchen, dining room, living room, office and hallway walls are gone. I made a master bedroom with its own bathroom. I had built-in desks, files and shelves made for our office."

Patnude picked up on "our office," but he didn't say anything.

"The kitchen has been remodeled and modernized, as have the bathrooms. The only room I didn't touch is your bedroom. It is exactly as I found it, maybe just as you left it."

Patnude was speechless, at least for a few seconds.

"I can't believe this is where I lived while I was growing up. I like it. Ma and Pa would love it. Ma was always complaining about the separate rooms. How did you do all this?"

"It was relatively easy and cheap to tear down the walls, none of them were loadbearing. Grandpa Boris and Seth helped with the teardowns. Do you like it?"

"I do like it. I can't believe it. Can I look into my old bedroom?"

Patnude followed Sissie into his old bedroom.

"This looks the same as the last time I saw it. It hasn't even been painted."

"Well, you can do whatever you want with it. It's your bedroom."

Patnude slipped behind Sissie and wrapped his arms around her waist as he started to kiss her gently around the neck and ear and started massaging her.

"What are you doing? You know the rules, if I'm making dinner no sex, Patnude."

"We haven't had dinner yet and I've always wanted to have sex in my old bedroom." Sissie turned around and started kissing him.

"Technically, you have a good point since we haven't had dinner yet," Sissie said, as she lowered herself onto the old wooden floor, pulling Patnude down on top of her.

Sissie and Patnude had a late Saturday night dinner, and Patnude realized he was no longer afraid to be in his old home. He was actually pleased, very pleased to be back—very pleased.

I.M. Receives the
Perfect Birthday Gift

Sissie was sitting quietly on the large couch in her living room, staring at the ceiling with a faraway look on her face.

"What are you thinking about?" Patnude asked.

"Has I.M. determined what Rolfer Sharper painted in his three paintings?"

"No, not yet. He mentions every now and then that he thinks he discovers what Rolfer painted, but then he comes back the following day with a depressed look and says he hasn't got it yet. He thinks it could be the same landscape scene that changes with the seasons, but it never quite works. Once in a while he's into cloud scenes, but his cloud interpretation always clouds up and disappears."

"My, aren't you clever with cloud scenes that cloud up and disappear. What if my birthday present to him was to sit down with him to describe and outline what Rolfer painted? Do you think he would like that? After all, it has been several months since he purchased them."

"I think that's a great idea. It would definitely make I.M.'s life less frustrating."

Famine had planned a surprise birthday party for I.M. Famine and Sissie were at I.M.'s house waiting for Patnude to bring him home. They both were wearing orange dresses, his cake was covered in orange frosting, his ice cream was orange flavored and his birthday candles were orange.

When I.M. walked through the door, Patnude, Sissie and Famine yelled, "Happy Birthday, I.M.!" He was surprised and pleased as he received hugs from everyone, even a manly hug from Patnude.

"Thank you, everything is in orange except for Patnude." Famine had gotten I.M.'s orange sport jacket out for him to wear.

After singing "Happy Birthday" and enjoying orange cake and ice cream, I.M. opened his gifts, all of which were wrapped in orange paper. Famine gave him an orange tie, shirt and belt. Each one was a slightly different shade of orange. I.M. had to put them on immediately and demanded or begged for Sissie to take pictures of him and Famine hugging each other.

Sissie gave I.M. a birthday card from her and Patnude. Inside the envelope was a little envelope. It was bright orange. The note inside the little orange envelope was written in orange ink on a white note card. It said, "Come with me and I will show you the secret of Rolfer's paintings."

Sissie motioned with her forefinger for I.M. to follow her into his dining room. He followed and sat down in the chair Sissie had pulled out at the far end of the dining room. Famine and Patnude followed. Sissie sat down alongside I.M. and pointed at the three paintings as she talked softly into I.M.'s ear.

She started with the red painting, the yellow and finally the orange painting and continued for about 10 minutes.

I.M. continued staring at the three Rolfer paintings.

"Well, I'll be damned, you're right Sissie. I can't believe I couldn't see it before. It was so simple. Once you decipher one painting, you can get the other two. Unbelievable. Thank you, Sissie."

Patnude still saw the same thing he always saw: three large paintings. One red, one yellow and one orange—nothing else.

Patnude and Sissie left I.M. and Famine sitting in his dining room looking at the three large Rolfer paintings in red, yellow and orange.

"You gave I.M. the perfect birthday gift," Patnude told Sissie on their short drive home.

Patnude Proposes in
His Own Way

"What are you going to do with your old bedroom? Remodel it? Repaint? Furnish? Move in?" Sissie asked.

Patnude nodded positively, "I was thinking all of the above."

"Were you now?"

"Yes, I was. We probably need to discuss terms, such as rent, privileges, availability of amenities and use of rooms."

"Hmm, lots of issues, sounds expensive. What kind of privileges were you interested in?"

"I would want the exclusive use of all rooms and the related amenities at all times on a long-term basis."

"Exclusive use of all amenities on a long-term basis?"

"Oh, yes and especially the amenities."

"Where are you planning on enjoying the amenities?"

"In your bedroom, where the amenities are frequently located, although they could be elsewhere from time to time."

"How long-term?"

"Hmm, I didn't think of an exact term. How about forever in the future?"

"Forever in the future with an exclusive contract that includes all amenities?"

"Yes, I think you got it."

"Well, let me think about it while you select my clothes for tomorrow. Oh, don't forget to shine my shoes. I'm going to bed now. If I'm sleeping when you come to bed, wake me gently and we can discuss your exclusive amenities privilege."

Tonight, Patnude was actually one step ahead of Sissie. He'd already selected her clothes and shined her shoes. He followed her into bed and put his arm around her and whispered into her ear, "Is this a good time to discuss the amenities?"

"It's a perfect time."

A Special Request from
Sissie and Famine

It was Wednesday night and Sissie and Famine were having dinner together. Patnude thought Sissie mentioned something about planning, he wasn't sure about what. Anyway, he was having dinner alone as he waited for Sissie. It was a little after 8:30 when Sissie walked in. She was wearing a bright orange sleeveless dress with orange ballet flats. She looked cute and spunky and, of course, sexy. She always ran up, hugged and kissed Patnude. Tonight's greeting kiss was a little more passionate than her usual greeting kiss. Patnude sensed she had something in mind.

"Hi, I am going to take a quick shower and get ready for bed. Let's go to bed early tonight so we can have a chat."

"How come you're dressed in all orange? You didn't invite I.M. did you?"

"No, just Famine and me. We decided to dress in orange tonight. Everyone at Le Citron thought we looked very cute getting in and out of our orange Mini Coopers."

Sissie finished her shower and grabbed Patnude's hand, pulling him to the couch. "Let's go to bed, we need to talk."

"You don't have any clothes on."

"I know. We are going to bed and when we finish talking we can do other things."

Patnude undressed and got into bed, and Sissie immediately rolled over alongside of him with her arm across his chest.

"Are you ready to talk?"

"Yes, I am."

"Good. Famine and I decided tonight that we should have a joint wedding. It will be cute, unusual and less costly. We haven't picked a date yet since we wanted to work out the date with you and I.M. What do you think?"

"Okay. You both were dressed in orange tonight? Is Famine telling I.M. tonight about the joint wedding? Are we done talking now and ready for other things?"

"Good, yes, yes and most definitely."

Thursday morning, Patnude was in his office waiting for I.M. They were driving down to Phoenix to pick up several coffins that I.M. got a deal on from a funeral home there. Since Maria was in the office every Thursday, it didn't take much of an excuse for I.M. to get out of the office.

Patnude heard Maria announce, "I found another one. Why doesn't he listen to me? Patnude, you aren't buying him blue pens, are you?"

Patnude didn't answer.

"Well, Patnude, are you?"

"No, Maria, I'm not," he answered as he checked his desk for any blue pens.

I.M. arrived and they were rather quickly off for Phoenix. As usual, Patnude was driving Best Funeral Home's new used Buick hearse.

"Maria found another one of your blue pens in, or on, your desk," Patnude stated.

"Damn it. I left it lying on top of my desk last night. I'm sure Maria threw it out. I forgot what day it was last night. I need to be more careful."

"How many coffins did you buy?"

"Four basic ones. We should be able to sell them pretty easily. I think they will just fit in our hearse, although it will be a tight fit. How do you like our new hearse?"

"It's okay."

"What do you think about Famine and Sissie's plan to have a joint wedding? It should cut our individual wedding expenses to almost half."

"I guess it's okay. I might have preferred a smaller, quieter wedding. In fact, a run-off and get married wouldn't be bad."

"A run-off wedding won't happen with either one of them."

"I know, I know, but one can always dream."

"We need to select a date and decide about our honeymoons. We can't both be gone at the same time."

"Good thought. Perhaps we could flip a coin to decide who gets the first five days off."

"What if we are swamped with deaths on that weekend?"

"I guess neither one of us gets a honeymoon until later."

"That could be a tough sell to Famine and Sissie."

"Most likely it will be. Maybe if we are swamped, we could send Sissie and Famine off together for a few days."

"That wouldn't be a honeymoon."

"No, you are right, that would not be a honeymoon."

"We could let Maria run the home for a few days, so that we each could have a honeymoon."

"I don't think so. Can you imagine what would happen if Maria found a blue pen on one of the deceased?"

"It wouldn't be pretty."

"No, it would not."

A Good Day Becomes A Bad Day

"**P**atnude, don't forget we're having dinner with Famine and I.M. tonight to discuss our wedding plans. I'll be at the funeral home by 6:00. Be careful today. I'll be in my office all day, so no need to worry about me." Sissie kissed Patnude on the lips and gave him a morning hug.

"You are dressed like a mortician today."

"Well, that's what I am," Patnude replied, as he walked down the stairs thinking how attractive Sissie was and that he'd rather be spending the day with her. "I'll check the hot water heater tonight. Don't you fool with it." Patnude saw the Sissie look that he didn't have a clue about hot water heaters. Sissie frequently gave him that look about many things.

Patnude was driving the hearse up to Show Low to pick up the body of Aveeno Laveen for burial at Forever Restful Cemetery. Aveeno was from Globe, but lived in Show Low for the last 10 years selling life insurance. The funeral service had already been held yesterday in Show Low, but the burial was going to be in Globe. Aveeno would be buried alongside his mother and father, who passed away about ten years ago.

In his younger days, Aveeno was known as "The Mailbox Killer." He would hang out of the right side of his brother's car and destroy mailboxes with his indestructible aluminum baseball bat. His older brother, Laddie, did the precise driving. They had plenty of practice and became a precision team in the drive-by act of destroying rural mailboxes. Aveeno and Laddie were well-known in the Globe-Miami area. The postal service never caught them, but the USPS was certainly aware of the rumors. After Aveeno moved up to Show Low, there was a drastic or almost elimination of the drive-by destruction of rural mailboxes. However, last Saturday night there was a rash of smashed and destroyed rural mailboxes in Show Low, which coincided with Laddie's trip while visiting his brother.

On Saturday night before Laddie was to return to Globe, Aveeno and Laddie were bar hopping. They'd left the Wild West Bar around midnight, and at about 1:00 a.m. Laddie had brought Aveeno to the Summit Healthcare Regional Medical Center. Aveeno had severe head injuries. It seemed they were reliving their youth by destroying rural mailboxes, when Aveeno's indestructible aluminum baseball bat bounced off a substantial mailbox and hit him in the head. He died a few hours later from severe head injuries.

Patnude understood why the prized indestructible aluminum baseball bat was lying alongside Aveeno in his coffin.

He had also heard that Aveeno had a substantial life insurance policy, whatever substantial means, and his brother Laddie was the sole beneficiary and would now be rich.

Patnude thought Aveeno qualified as a *Globe-Miami resident.*

He picked up the closed casket from the Show Low funeral home. Before Patnude left for Globe, Laddie asked if he could ride back with him so he could have one last ride with his brother.

"It was a perfect vacation with Aveeno until Saturday night," Laddie said.

Patnude just nodded as he headed south towards Globe on U.S. Route 60.

"I should have never let Aveeno talk me into activating our mailbox killer routine again. I don't know what I was thinking. Too many drinks, and Aveeno could be very persuasive. I guess that's why he was a life insurance salesman. I don't know what's going to happen with the USPS. I hope nothing, since I was only driving. I guess now I'm going to be rich from Aveeno's life insurance, but I will miss him."

Patnude kept driving as he listened to Laddie. He was looking forward to tonight's dinner with Sissie, I.M. and Famine at Le Citron. It sounded interesting to plan their joint wedding ceremony, but most likely it would be he and I.M. agreeing to Sissie and Famine's wedding plans. Nevertheless, it would be an enjoyable dinner.

The burial service for Aveeno was scheduled for tomorrow. After he dropped Laddie off at his house, he headed to Best Funeral Home.

As Patnude backed up the hearse into the garage, he noticed Sissie's orange Mini Cooper wasn't there yet, Famine's was there, as were several other cars he didn't recognize. After parking and unloading Aveeno Laveen, he walked into Best Funeral Home's office and found I.M., Famine, Grandpa Boris and Seth Ostler talking amongst themselves. They looked serious and stopped talking when they saw him walk in.

"Hello, Patnude," I.M. said. Why don't you sit down, we have something we need to tell you."

Patnude followed I.M.'s instructions and as he was sitting down he asked, "Where's Sissie?"

"Sissie was killed late morning or early afternoon when the gas hot water heater exploded, setting the building on fire. Sissie would have been killed instantly from the explosion. The subsequent fire destroyed her body and the building. Her body wasn't found until the firemen were going through the ash and rubble of the building. Her body is now at the hospital. I'm so sorry to be the one to have to tell you this. Tonight was going to be a celebration dinner."

I.M. leaned over and hugged Patnude.

"Can I go see her body?"

Grandpa Boris stepped forward.

"Patnude, I saw her remains at the hospital. Sissie would not want anyone seeing her looking like she does. You wouldn't recognize her. I didn't. She would not want you looking at her like she is now. Just remember her as she was."

Patnude nodded, yes. "I understand, Grandpa Boris. I told her this morning not to fool around with the hot water heater, and to let me do it tonight. She gave me one of her Sissie looks. I knew she was going to fool with it, but I couldn't have stopped her. What am I going to do without her?"

Famine hugged Patnude as she sat down alongside of him. "We all need to have dinner tonight and tell Sissie stories, which we all will have. You can ride with I.M. and me."

Dinner was sad, happy and long with everybody telling their Sissie stories. Patnude already knew, but now fully realized the effect Sissie had on family, friends and him. Sissie was someone special. He would miss her special looks and even her dope slaps, which he thought she enjoyed too much.

Patnude drove home and was alone in his apartment for the first time in a while. After his shower, he sat on his living room couch looking at photos of Sissie. He was listening to music from the 1940s. Sissie liked to listen to the 1940s music late in the evening, which meant he also did, and in reality, he really did enjoy listening to the 1940s music. Sissie always looked happy and caring in her photos, and also had an air of sexiness. The photo he was looking at was of him and Sissie dancing. He could almost feel her arms holding him, smell her perfume and see her warm loving expression.

He suddenly became aware of the song playing on the 1940s radio station. It was Vera Lynn's, *We'll Meet Again*. The opening lyrics brought tears to his eyes.

> *"We'll meet again*
> *Don't know where*
> *Don't know when*
> *But I know we'll meet again some sunny day*
> *Keep smiling through*
> *Just like you always do*
> *'Til the blue skies drive the dark clouds away"*

When Vera Lynn finished *We'll Meet Again*, he turned the radio off, laid down on the couch holding the photo of Sissie and fell asleep missing her.

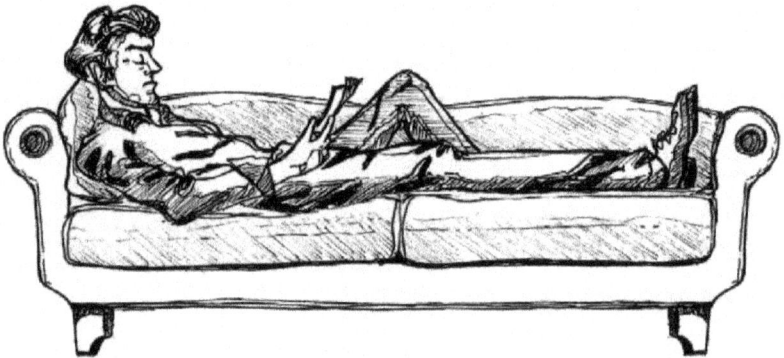

Sissie Helps Patnude
Become More Compassionate

Patnude was reading the obituaries, a daily and mandatory requirement for a mortician.

He saw Sissie's obituary with her picture and the usual bio and funeral information. The photograph represented her well. The reader could easily feel how special she was. The words struck him hard as he began to accept that everything related to Sissie was now past-tense. He'd never thought of Sissie in the past-tense before. His feelings and thoughts had always been in relation to the present and future. He knew Sissie was past-tense, but his feelings and emotions were struggling with Sissie in the past-tense. It was a hard pill to swallow.

Patnude realized he'd had no trouble accepting all of the other people reported in the obituaries as past-tense—what else could they be? The same applied to all of the deceased serviced by Best Funeral Home. They were all dead and accepted by him as being dead, period. End of discussion. Perhaps he'd been too cold or reserved with the deceased's survivors. He'd always tried to be respectful and understanding, but maybe he lacked compassion for their loss of a loved one.

Patnude decided, then and there, that he needed to be more compassionate and understanding when someone lost a loved one. To realize they are having a new experience, that their loved one was now past-tense. Nothing happens in the future for the departed, and only memories from now on for the survivors.

He would strive to be more compassionate from now on. Patnude then felt a loving and gentle dope slap on his right cheek—from Sissie?

Sissie's Gone

I.M., Grandpa Boris and Famine handled everything regarding Sissie's funeral and burial service, both of which were well attended. As expected, her coffin was closed, and there were several framed photographs of her on display.

Patnude was surprised, but not really, on how many people paid their respects to Sissie. She was a unique person.

He knew how lucky he'd been to have known her and to have loved her. There would never be another Sissie. Patnude didn't cry at either the funeral or burial service. He felt sad, solemn, depressed, and maybe a little angry—but he realized he didn't feel alone because he could still feel Sissie in his life. How strange that he could still sense and feel her presence even after she was buried. How strange.

After the funeral, Patnude asked Grandpa Boris, "What about Sissie's mother? Is she coming to pay her respects?"

"I don't think so since there would be no money in it for her. I called and left a message at the last phone number I had for Brendie and she hasn't called me back. She didn't do anything when Sweenie died, except ask if there was any inheritance for her. I would be surprised if she calls me back. I don't think Sissie would want Brendie at her funeral."

"I don't understand her attitude."

"She really is quite easy to understand. She is a self-centered, greedy bitch that only thinks of herself."

"Hard to believe she is Sissie's mother."

"That's what Sweenie and I said many times over the years."

I.M. had ordered Patnude to take the week off after Sissie's death. Famine called him every day, as did Grandpa Boris. The following week, Patnude collected all of her clothes and personal items from his apartment and organized them to give to charity. He hadn't realized that she'd left her blue T and A dress in his closet. He couldn't give that away. He could still picture her in that dress tantalizing him with her charms. All of her shoes were polished and detailed to perfection. Sissie would have been, or maybe is, proud of him as he boxed them up for charity. He looked at her blue T and A dress again and could remember her leaning across the table with her arm out-stretched holding her glass of wine to make a toast. She'd leaned over so a good portion of her breasts were exposed. He could hear her say "to us" as she clinked her glass with his three times. He still felt her in his life, and this pleased him. Patnude fell asleep smiling to himself, as once again his thoughts were of Sissie.

Back to Normal

Patnude was driving the new used Buick hearse and I.M. was in the passenger seat. Keeto Cooper was riding in the back inside his coffin. They were driving to Forever Restful Cemetery for Keeto Cooper's burial service.

"What was Keeto doing up on a power pole during a thunderstorm?" Patnude asked.

"Clara told me he had a theory that he could catch the electrical power from lightning and store it in batteries for future use. He'd climb the power pole at the back of their house while holding a copper rod that was connected to batteries. He held the rod up high in order to catch the lightning, so it would then transfer the electrical power to the attached batteries."

"You're kidding."

"No, I'm not. Clara told me he'd been doing this for several years. She said he would struggle to climb the power pole with those spikes attached to his shoes and ankles. He would climb to the very top and hold his long copper rod up, hoping to catch a thunderbolt. Clara also said Keeto was usually drinking when he decided to try and catch the thunderbolt."

"Is lightning what killed Keeto?"

"Not directly. Clara said lightning struck a large pine tree not far from the pole Keeto climbed. The crash of the nearby thunderbolt must have scared him, as he dropped his copper rod across the power lines, which shorted out the electrical system. As he leaned back, his safety belt wasn't fastened correctly, and he fell off of the power pole onto his head. To add insult to injury, the copper rod he was holding fell and impaled him through his abdomen as he lay on the ground, then lightning struck the long copper rod which was now stuck through Keeto. Initially there were some questions about what actually killed him. Was it the fall, the copper rod impalement, the lightning strike, or all three? I don't think Keeto could have survived any one of them. Therefore, I think the fall did it, and the impalement and lightning strike were just extras to ensure that Keeto was really dead."

"You are probably right. What did Keeto do for a living?"

"He was a safety engineer."

"How is Clara doing?"

"She seems to be okay, but is angry at Keeto for doing something so stupid that it killed him. She says she warned him hundreds of times, but he wouldn't listen to her, especially when he was drinking during a thunderstorm. I guess in reality, she is more mad than sad."

"That's too bad, but I can understand."

"Me too."

"After Keeto's service, I want to stop by Sissie's gravesite for a minute. I want to check her headstone."

"Okay, she is buried next to Grandma Sweenie, isn't she?"

"Yes, she is."

"How are you doing?"

"I'm doing better. Still sad and miss Sissie a lot and think of her frequently, but I'm glad I met her and got to spend time with her."

"As I told you, Sissie was one in a million."

Rinny Comes Home to Carmine

Patnude was working in his office when he thought he heard Carmine Rightful in the reception area talking with Maria. He didn't think this would turn out well.

"Butcher Jim told me he saw my cat, Rinny, in your office," Carmine said rather calmly.

"It's none of your business what I have in my office," Maria replied as she tried to slowly and discreetly close her office door.

"Are you trying to close your office door?" Carmine asked. "You must have my Rinny."

"I'll close my door if I want to. I don't want you in my office. You understand?" Maria commented.

Carmine was dressed like the new Carmine and not the old Carmine. She looked a little slimmer. Her hair was even a more mellow red and styled. Her lipstick was a softer red and neatly applied.

"Hello, Carmine, how are you? You look very nice today."

"Patnude, I was very sorry to hear about Sissie. I met her several times and she was very nice to me. Not like this bitch Maria, who stole my cat Rinny. I want my Rinny back now."

Carmine headed towards Maria's office.

Maria was standing in front of her office door in a vertical spread eagle pose. Carmine put her hands on each side of Maria's waist, lifted her up and out of the way and opened Maria's office door.

"There's my Rinny. You did steal her! You bitch!" Carmine walked directly to the shelf behind Maria's desk and grabbed her Rinny.

Maria was standing in shock in the exact spot where Carmine had set her down. As Carmine walked by Maria she said, "She doesn't look too bad, plus her eyes are glued back in."

Maria unfroze and went to grab Rinny, but Carmine pushed her away. However, Maria was able to grab Rinny's tail, which ripped off as Carmine walked towards the door of Best Funeral Home's office.

"You can keep Rinny's tail as a fond memory of her," Carmine shouted at Maria.

Carmine softly said to Patnude as she walked by him, "I forgot to tell you that Butcher Jim and I are dating. It might get serious."

Maria was frozen holding and staring at Rinny's ripped off tail.

Patnude's first thought was that Derwood Sloan must have done a good job at re-gluing Rinny's eyes back in; but just then the left eye popped out and rolled towards him. Carmine was squeezing Rinny's head again. Patnude picked up the eye and handed it to her.

"Thank you," Carmine said politely, as she then gave Maria the evil eye. She left Best Funeral Home's office with Rinny's head held in her right hand and Rinny's left eye held in her left hand.

Patnude's second thought was *just another day here in Globe, Arizona.*

The Death of Waldon Wackenhut, A Great Accountant

It was 10:30 on Tuesday morning when I.M. walked into Patnude's office. He looked gloomy. Not a good look for a mortician. He didn't say anything as he stared at Patnude.

"What's wrong?" Patnude asked.

"Wally Wackenhut died yesterday. We have to go to the hospital to pick up his body later this afternoon."

"Isn't, or wasn't Wally your accountant?"

"Yes. He was preparing Best Funeral Home's tax return which is due next week. I don't know where he was with the return. I called his office, but Jill hasn't returned my call yet. Let's go right after lunch to pick up his body."

"Wally wasn't that old. What did he die of?"

"Too much vodka, a bad heart and an aneurysm in his brain that burst. He was found dead slumped over his desk holding an empty bottle of vodka in his right hand. He was only 53."

Patnude was driving the new used Buick hearse to pick up Wally Wackenhut and I.M. was on his cell phone.

"Thanks for the info, Jill. I will pick up Best's income tax return and records later this week. Thanks, again."

"Good news?" Patnude asked.

"Yes, you're not going to believe this. Wally finished and signed Best's income tax return before he died! He ran all of his client billings up to date, answered all of his e-mails and phone messages, signed all of his correspondence, prepared a to-do list, finished his bottle of vodka and then died."

"I guess one could call Wally a good accountant and maybe even a great one."

"Wally was a great accountant."

"Was Maria still having an affair with him?"

"I think they were still lovers, although it's hard for me to think of anybody being Maria's lover. I bet she has a printed list of rules and procedures for a lover to follow, and God forbid if he has a blue pen."

"Wasn't Maria's ex-husband an accountant?"

"Yes, he is or was a competitor of Wally Wackenhut. Shamsie Gentle was an aggressive competitor of Wally's. That's probably why Maria selected Wally as a lover."

"I guess Maria likes accountants."

"It appears she does."

Wally Wackenhut was tall, skinny and easy to lift in and out of the hearse. His viewing was scheduled for Thursday with burial service late that afternoon. Wally was an easy prep since he didn't have any external physical damage, and he was light to move around. Patnude and I.M. dressed him in a typical accountant's dark blue suit, white shirt, red tie, and large horn-rimmed glasses. Wally looked like a sleeping, well-dressed accountant, although neither I.M. or Patnude could ever remember him in a suit.

Maria was dressed in black when she came in Wednesday afternoon to pay her respects in private to Wally Wackenhut. She wasn't crying, as there were no tears, but she had a distraught look on her face.

"How could Wally die? He was so young," she told Patnude, as she stood next to the coffin with her right hand on Wally's shoulder.

"I will miss him. We were pretty close. He was so young. I told him a hundred times to quit drinking vodka, but he never listened. I'll miss my Wally."

Thursday morning at 10:00, Waldon Wackenhut's viewing commenced. The first person to attend was his main competitor and Maria's ex-husband, Shamsie Gentle. In fact, Shamsie was there for the entire viewing and subsequent burial service. He greeted everyone who attended and gave each one of them his business card. It was a great new client marketing day for Shamsie, maybe his greatest. An opportunity like the death of a competitor doesn't come along very often.

Maria was furious when she saw what Shamsie was doing. In fact, she started to lecture Patnude that he should throw Shamsie out when I.M. interrupted her and told Maria that he just engaged Shamsie as Best Funeral Home's accountant and tax return preparer.

Maria turned bright red and started stammering, "You can't, you didn't, how could you, I can't deal with him, do you see what he is doing, why, and what am I going to do?"

"You are going to have to learn to deal with Shamsie. It shouldn't be that hard," I.M. answered.

"Well I can't and won't," Maria said as she stormed back to her office.

I.M. and Patnude assumed she was cleaning out her desk and looking, for the last time, for any of I.M.'s hidden caches of blue pens.

Patnude and I.M. didn't see Maria again until they got to Wally's gravesite at Forever Restful Cemetery. They stared with their mouths open as they saw Maria get out of Shamsie's car and walk arm in arm up to the gravesite.

Patnude commented, "Maria is more flexible with accountants, ex-husbands and maybe future lovers than she is with blue pens."

"It appears so," I.M. replied.

Another Day at
Best Funeral Home

Patnude and I.M. were on their way to pick up the body of Speedy Short from Mountain Top Assisted Living Center.

"How old was Speedy?" Patnude asked as he drove the new used Buick hearse, cautiously as always.

"He was 79. He died on his birthday, Memorial Day right after the Indy 500 was completed."

"He was a race car fan, wasn't he?"

"My, oh my. Yes, he was. He always wanted to have the fastest car in the Globe-Miami area and many times he did. Speedy had his electric mobility scooter modified so that it was the fastest electric scooter at the Mountain Top Assisted Living Center. He was warned many times by the center to slow down and be cautious."

"Did he slow down?"

"Only until security walked or turned away. A few times he would get behind a fellow resident who was in a wheelchair and push them fast."

"Inside or outside?"

"Both."

"Did he ever have accidents?"

"Oh, yes. Several fellow residents rammed the wall at the end of the hallway. Of course, his apartment door and walls had holes in them. His furniture was busted up and some had missing legs. All the moldings were ripped off the apartment's door jambs. He was the electric scooter terror of Mountain Top Assisted Living Center."

"He fell off the second-floor open deck into the pool, didn't he?"

"Well, not exactly. Speedy was racing another electric scooter down the second-floor hallway, and of course he was winning. His racing competitor slowed down and stopped when she realized she was losing, or more accurately lost the race.

Speedy kept going full speed ahead down the hallway. He crashed through the swinging doors that led into the game room. He rammed several card tables and flew through the sliding screen door that led onto the second-floor deck and crashed through the railing onto the pool deck. Speedy was still riding his electric scooter as it finally slid to a stop alongside the deep end of the pool. Speedy crouched over to disconnect the extra battery on the floor of the scooter, which he held in place with his legs and feet. He tried to release the battery and it is assumed that he grabbed the positive and negative cables with each hand. The electric scooter shot forward into the pool. Speedy hit his head against the diving board and subsequently sank to the bottom of the pool and drowned."

"Well, what killed Speedy?"

"The police weren't sure. He could have been electrocuted, which caused him to drive into the water, or perhaps hitting his head against the diving board, which also could have killed him. But, we know for sure he could not have survived drowning. So, I guess Speedy's death was an electrocution, crash collision and drowning. He might have been able to survive one or two of the above, but not all three."

"Does Speedy have any family?"

"No, they are all deceased. His son, Speedy Jr., was killed about 20 years ago in a motorcycle/horse accident in Douglas."

"Speedy Jr. was driving the motorcycle?"

"No, he was actually riding the horse when a speeding motorcycle hit him and the horse. The horse lived, and Speedy Jr. and the motorcyclist died at the scene of the accident."

"What happened to Mrs. Short?"

"Inky divorced Speedy years ago and remarried. He husband passed away and she lives at the Mountain Top Assisted Living Center. You are not going to believe this, but Inky was the woman racing Speedy down the hallway."

"So Inky is the sole survivor of the family."

"It appears so."

"What was Speedy's real first name?"

"Mowat. However, I don't believe anybody ever called him Mowat. He was always known as Speedy."

"Well, at least he died doing something he liked to do, winning an electric scooter race against his ex-wife. Will Speedy's casket be open?"

"I believe so. I think we can cover up the head damage from striking the pool's diving board. Maybe his hands are burnt from grabbing the battery cables."

"I suspect Mountain Top is glad that Speedy is no longer a resident."

"Yes, I would think so. Speedy had 'driving too fast' issues his entire life."

Patnude and I.M. picked up the body of Speedy Short and headed back to Best Funeral Home.

"I told you Speedy would have an open casket. Did you want to stop and grab a coffee at the drive-thru?" I.M. asked.

"No, Maria will be in this morning and I left a note for her to make a fresh pot."

"Do you think she will?"

"Maybe."

"Okay. I am going to toss my blue pen into the glove compartment so that Maria doesn't catch me with it. Don't let me forget it."

Patnude pulled the new used Buick hearse into the back parking lot and backed it up into the rear entrance of the funeral home.

"Isn't that Shamsie Gentle's car parked next to Maria's car? I thought he only came in at the end of each quarter?" Patnude asked.

"Yes, it is. I don't know what he is doing here. What's Carmine Rightful doing looking into Maria's back office window?"

"She probably decided she wanted Rinny's tail back."

Before they could unload Speedy Short's body, Carmine looked at them and waved.

"What is she doing? She is holding her cell phone against Maria's window and smiling. Why is she smiling?" Patnude questioned himself and I.M.

"I don't know. Maybe Maria is working really hard. Who knows?" I.M. replied while in the process of unlocking Best Funeral Home's back door.

Patnude saw and heard Carmine rap lightly on Maria's office window while holding up her cell phone with her other hand. She walked towards Patnude with a big smile on her face. Patnude wasn't sure he ever saw Carmine with that big of a smile ever before.

"Hi, Carmine. You look very nice today. Is that a new dress?" Patnude asked.

"Thank you. Yes, it is. Carmi selected it for me, she has such good taste and always knows what's in style. She also picked out my shoes. Carmi is becoming my best friend and we both are enjoying telling Kipfer what to do. We make a good team."

"I have my check for the changes we made to my coffin, but I wanted to give it directly to Maria, but she has both the front and back doors locked. That's not good for business, even I know that."

As I.M. unlocked the back door, he thought he heard Maria's office door close and then lock.

"Maria is meeting with Shamsie on top of her desk and I have the photos right here on my cell phone," Carmine gleefully announced to I.M. and Patnude.

I.M. walked back to Maria's office, tried to open door, but it was locked. He knocked on the frosted glass door window.

"Maria, open your office door. Carmine Rightful is here to make a payment."

"Just a minute, I'm in the middle of a meeting with Shamsie," Maria replied.

It took Maria a little over a minute to open the door. By then, Carmine was standing alongside I.M. with her check made payable to Best Funeral Home in her hand. Carmine continued smiling like a cat that swallowed the canary. Maria looked somewhat disheveled, her lipstick was smeared, her hair was rumpled, and her skirt and blouse were tousled. Shamsie was sitting in front of Maria's desk with his legs crossed, his hair neatly combed, but of course he wore a crewcut. However, he wasn't wearing any socks.

"Hi Maria," Carmine said most pleasantly. "I have my check for the changes I made to my coffin a few weeks ago. I would like a receipt, please."

Maria didn't say anything as she grabbed Carmine's check and walked back to her desk in a huff.

"Maria, your blouse is untucked in the back. Hi, Shamsie, how are you? Not wearing socks these days? Be careful of blisters."

Maria rushed writing the receipt and handed it to Carmine.

"Thank you. Oh, look there's my Rinny's tail on your bookshelf. She wants it back," Carmine said as she grabbed the tail off the bookshelf. "Oh, by the way, if you give me your e-mail address I have a few arousing photos of you and Shamsie that both you and your fellow Globe residents will enjoy. Thanks again for Rinny's tail." Carmine smilingly said as she left Maria's office. Maria and Shamsie's mouths fell open. I.M. had a small positive smile since he thought he now might be able to negotiate the use of his blue pens with Maria.

Patnude missed all of the above since he was unloading Speedy Short's body from the new used Buick hearse. However, as Carmine walked by Patnude she said, "See you, and check your e-mails for some entertaining and enlightening photos."

He realized Carmine had a sly, satisfied look on her face as she walked by him and then I.M. walked up to help him with Speedy's body and he had an even more sly look. He then heard Maria's office door slam shut, breaking the door's glass window.

An unusual afternoon, but after all, this is Globe, Arizona.

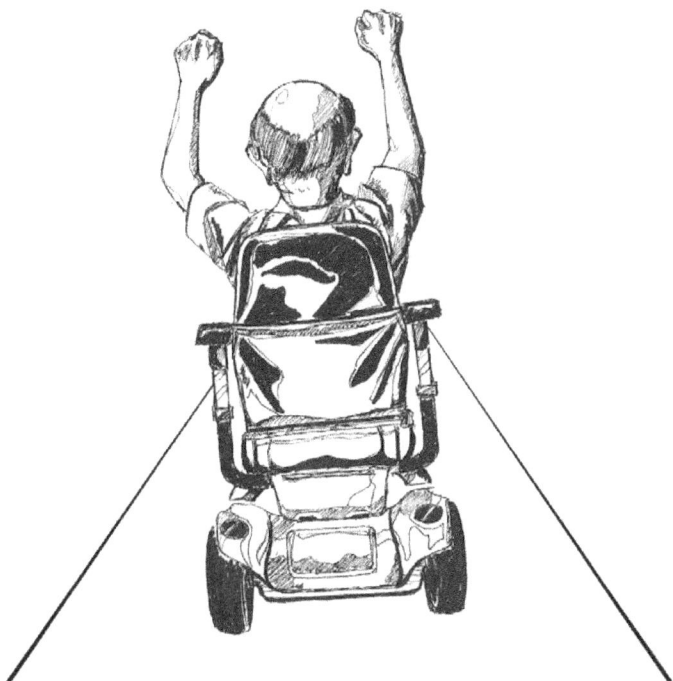

Patnude Begins Again

Patnude was sitting in his and Sissie's favorite coffee shop in Globe, except there was no longer a Sissie. He couldn't believe how much he loved and missed her. He could still see her sitting across from him in her provocative blue dress that caught every male's attention—including his own. When she got up to leave the coffee shop, the eyes of all the males in the shop followed her, including Patnude's. She always looked back and smiled at him. He did miss her. Why did she have to fool around with that water heater? At least her death was quick and painless. Patnude slowly sipped his coffee as he held the cup tightly with both hands.

"Patnude, how are you? May I join you? I was very sad to hear about Sissie's death. She was a lovely person. You have my deepest sympathy."

Patnude looked up; it was Jackie Snow. He hadn't seen her since the liver and onions dinner with I.M. and Famine about a year ago or so.

"Hi, Jackie, thank you for your thoughts. Yes, please sit down and join me. How are you?"

"I'm fine. You didn't answer my question. How are you?"

"I think I'm okay, but I miss Sissie and certainly feel alone now."

"How long has it been since the accident?"

"A little over a month."

"Are you back working now?"

"Yes, I am. I only took a week off. I.M. is very considerate and treats me like family. Plus, he keeps me busy, and he and Famine frequently have me over for dinner."

"Well, I'll tell you what I'm going to do. You and I are going out to dinner tonight. If you have other plans, cancel them. I just closed a big contract this morning and need someone to celebrate with. Besides, you helped me when my brother Johnny was killed in his motorcycle accident. Plus, I'm buying, but you have to drive and pick me up. You know, just a female thing. Are you still driving your white Chevrolet Impala?"

"Yes, I am, but I don't know if I'm a good dinner companion."

Just then Patnude felt his right cheek stinging as if someone slapped him. Then it happened three more times. Patnude was rubbing his right cheek that hurt like when Sissie was giving him dope slaps. There was another slap and more stinging.

Jackie watched as Patnude got a strange shocked look on his face as he continued to rub his right cheek.

"Is anything wrong?" asked Jackie.

"No, nothing is wrong, my cheek just felt a little unusual."

"Well, what about dinner tonight?"

"Well...I don't..." Patnude felt another hard dope slap to his right cheek. It stung. He looked around as he continued to rub his right cheek. He wondered what was happening.

"Patnude, you need to have dinner with me tonight."

"Okay, I will have dinner with you tonight."

"Good! Dress casually, like me. I don't want you wearing your mortician suit. Something like I'm wearing will be fine. Pick me up at 6:45. Here is my card with my home address on the back, in case you forgot where I live. I'll tell you where we are going when you pick me up. Again, dress casually and be on time, understand?"

"I understand, dress casually, like you, and don't be late."

"Good, see you at 6:45." Jackie touched Patnude's hand and held it for a few seconds, before turning around and walking out of the coffee shop.

Patnude forgot how attractive Jackie was and she didn't look sad anymore. He also noted her casual outfit of tan slacks, blue blazer, men's light blue long-sleeved shirt with a button-down collar and dark brown penny loafers. He thought he could match it. All of a sudden, he was looking forward to tonight's dinner with Jackie Snow and his right cheek had stopped stinging.

I.M. and His Chocolate Frosted Cake Donut

I.M. was sitting at his desk, reviewing the checks he'd just signed. It was the end of the month and the bills needed to be paid. As he reviewed this month's revenues, he sipped his hot cup of coffee while taking teeny nibbles from his chocolate frosted cake donut. He wanted the chocolate frosted cake donut to last as long as possible.

As president and owner of Best Funeral Home, I.M. confirmed it was another good month since they'd had 15 viewings, 10 of which included burial services. It certainly was one of their best months. He always enjoyed using the word "best" in relation to Best Funeral Home. He smiled to himself, as he thought, *sometimes it doesn't take much to entertain himself, and after all his last name is Best.* Which then reminded him of the story his father told him about how the Best family got their name.

When his grandfather immigrated to America and was being processed through Ellis Island, the government immigration officer asked him for his last name. Before answering, his grandfather looked up and saw the sign, "Be Your Best in America," after which he replied to the officer, "My last name is Best." I.M. enjoyed the story every time his father told it, especially when he ended with the words, "Always be your Best."

I.M. took another sip of his coffee, which was cooling down, and took a full bite of his chocolate frosted donut. He found it difficult to merely nibble at it.

He double checked his signature on the checks he'd just signed to confirm he'd used a black pen. He breathed a sigh of relief. Maria would have gone nuts if he had used one of his secret blue pens. He looked down and saw he had about half of his chocolate frosted cake donut remaining. I.M. couldn't resist any longer and picked it up and stuffed it into his mouth as Patnude walked into his office.

"You know you should buy chocolate frosted cake donut holes," Patnude advised.

Dinner with Jackie Snow

Patnude parked in front of Jackie Snow's house at 6:42 and knocked on her door at exactly 6:45. She opened her door on the fourth knock.

"Wow, you're exactly on time, and no longer in your mortician suit!" Jackie exclaimed. "And of course, you are driving your white Chevy."

Patnude was wearing tan slacks, a blue blazer, a light blue shirt with a button-down collar and dark brown penny loafers.

Jackie laughed as she looked Patnude over. "You follow instructions very well. I guess it was a good thing that I wasn't wearing a dress when we met in the coffee shop."

Jackie still had on the same clothes she was wearing when they met in the coffee shop earlier in the day.

"We look like twins, don't you think? How unique. Let's see if we get any comments from anyone."

Jackie had selected an Italian restaurant for her celebration dinner; however she decided salad, pizza and a bottle of red Italian wine would be perfect for them.

"Tell me what we are celebrating," Patnude asked.

"I sold a used MRI machine to a medical practice in Mesa. I have been marketing to them for over six months and had almost given up, but thank goodness I didn't."

"Congratulations. Do you do a lot of traveling?"

"Yes, I cover Arizona, New Mexico, Colorado, Nevada and sometimes Southern California. I'm out of town most of the time."

"Have you had liver and onions since our dinner with I.M. and Famine?"

"I have, in fact three or four times. How about you?"

"No, never again, I don't like liver and onions."

"Were you and Sissie getting serious? Do they still say that?"

"Yes, we were. It was a tragic shock when she was killed in the explosion and fire. I told her not to fool around with the gas hot water heater, but Sissie was very independent and did what she wanted. I miss her and think of her frequently."

"How sad, I knew Sissie a little bit and liked her. I think the feeling was mutual. It will just take time for you to heal."

Jackie and Patnude chatted as they ate their salad and pizza and drank their red Italian wine.

Patnude walked Jackie to her door. They shook hands and then Jackie gave him a hug.

"Thanks for going out to dinner with me, I enjoyed your company. Next time I'm back in town, I will give you a call and you can take me out to dinner."

"Good night, Jackie, thanks for dinner and everything. I appreciate your thoughts and concerns."

As he drove home, Patnude thought about how nice and caring Jackie was, and that under different circumstances, they'd have done more than just shake hands good night. Maybe later, who knows?

Triple S' Funeral with A Twist

Patnude hadn't done his get-out-of-town weekend in three or four months. For some reason his didn't feel like getting out of town, at least not now. He actually worked, since Best Funeral Home always seemed to have funerals. It was early Thursday morning before the scheduled viewing of Schafer S. Schafer. This was an open casket funeral since Schafer S. Schafer, known around Globe as Triple S, shot himself in the heart while cleaning his unloaded hunting rifle. At least that is what his widow claimed, and the police so far have accepted her story. Although some local Globe residents questioned the incident, as Triple S and Mrs. Schafer had started divorce proceedings. Triple S was dating Myntz, a much younger woman. Triple S had taught gun safety classes around Globe for many years. Myntz was convinced that Mrs. Schafer shot Triple S and she started to carry a pistol for protection.

Patnude thought this was normal for Globe, Arizona.

I.M. walked into Patnude's office. "How about a cup of coffee? I'll pour." I.M. was carrying Best Funeral Home's coffee pot.

"Yes, please," Patnude answered.

"Patnude, you haven't taken a get-out-of-town weekend since Sissie died."

"I know, I just haven't felt like leaving town. I don't mind just hanging around."

"I see. Well, Famine and I have decided this is your get-out-of-town weekend and you are getting out of town. We booked you a room at the Valley Ho in Scottsdale for the weekend and paid for it. We want you out of town tomorrow morning and not to return until Monday afternoon. That's an order and your only answer is yes."

Patnude smiled and started to ask a question, and before he could speak, I.M. repeated, "Your only answer is yes."

"Thank you and thank Famine also."

The viewing of Triple S started promptly at 10:00 a.m. Patnude was a little surprised that Mrs. Schafer wasn't in attendance at the start of the viewing. Many of the attendees at the viewing were gun enthusiast friends. Myntz arrived at 10:30 and she had an automatic pistol holstered and strapped to her right side. Patnude overheard several of the attendees saying that they couldn't believe that Triple S shot himself with a loaded gun while he was cleaning it. They exclaimed he was a safety freak who always checked and rechecked that the gun was empty whenever he was finished shooting or before he cleaned it. No way could he have shot himself cleaning a loaded rifle. Myntz stood alongside Triple S' casket for almost an hour just looking at him.

Myntz looked to be in her late twenties or early thirties, attractive and in good shape and appeared to be an outdoorsy person, whatever that is. Everyone was gone by 2:30 and it was just Patnude and the corpse of Triple S when Mrs. Schafer walked in. She was most likely an attractive woman many years ago. She stumbled and weaved as she walked up to Triple S' casket. Patnude could tell she had been drinking.

"I want to be alone with my husband if you don't mind," she said to Patnude.

"I understand," he replied as he stepped out of the viewing room.

Patnude watched Mrs. Schafer through one of the security system cameras.

Mrs. Schafer grabbed the lapels of Triple S' dark blue suit and raised him slightly as she started to shake him. She was mumbling something Patnude couldn't hear. The she screamed, "You dumb son of a bitch. You prick bastard. You stopped making payments on your life insurance policy and it lapsed. I would have never shot you if I knew you didn't have life insurance. You probably spent the money for the life insurance premiums on that tramp, Myntz. I hope she gave you V.D. You bastard. What am I going to do now?"

Mrs. Schafer then released Triple S' suit lapels and let him fall back into his casket. She turned around and quickly walked out of Best Funeral Home.

Patnude called Sergeant Peterson of the Globe Police Department as soon as Mrs. Schafer pulled out of the parking lot.

Sergeant Peterson watched the recording of Mrs. Schafer and her conversation with the deceased Triple S at least six times.

"I could not believe that Triple S accidentally shot himself while cleaning his rifle. He was always the safety freak. Send copies of Mrs. Schafer's comments to these e-mail addresses and write a memo describing what you saw and heard. Also, save the recording. Thanks, Patnude."

As Patnude was writing his memo for Sergeant Peterson, his mind drifted to the possibility of the prior deceased at Best Funeral Home actually being murder victims, with the murderers still free. This thought frightened him.

Patnude's Get-Out-of-Town Long Weekend

Friday morning I.M. and Famine almost escorted Patnude out of town. Grandpa Boris had given him Sissie's orange Mini Cooper S as a gift. It was a lot more exciting than his white 4-door Chevrolet Impala or Best Funeral Home's new used Buick hearse.

I.M. and Famine ordered him, "To get out of town and don't come back until Monday afternoon."

It was a fun drive in the Mini down to Scottsdale. Patnude checked into the Hotel Valley Ho after lunch. He wasn't sure what he was going to, do but decided to walk around Old Town Scottsdale for the afternoon.

After dinner, he was sitting by the pool in his swim trunks when he heard a loud female voice say, "Is that you Patnude?"

He looked up and saw Carmine Rightful and Butcher Jim standing in front of him, holding drinks.

Carmine still had bright red hair, but toned down and styled, her lipstick was bright red, but neatly applied and she looked thinner—much thinner, but still a big woman. She looked happy, as did Butcher Jim.

"What are you two doing in Scottsdale?" Patnude asked.

"We needed a weekend away together, and now that Butcher Jim has hired help at his butcher shop, we took advantage of the opportunity."

"What are you doing in Scottsdale?"

"Same thing you are."

Patnude looked up and noticed an attractive woman getting out of the pool, who grabbed a towel and walked towards them. He admired her nice long legs as she stopped in front of them.

"May I join you?" she asked.

"Of course," Carmine answered.

"Patnude you know Jackie Snow, don't you?"

Patnude was speechless for a few moments as he looked at Jackie in her bathing suit.

"Well Patnude, do you know Jackie or not?" Carmine asked.

"Well Patnude, do you know me?"

"Yes, of course, I just didn't recognize you in your swimsuit. You're usually wearing slacks, and a blazer, with penny loafers."

Jackie smiled and answered, "Well now you will be able to remember me in two different outfits," as she pulled out a chair and sat next to him.

The foursome chatted for about a half hour about Globe and themselves.

"Whatever happened to your tailless Rinny?" Patnude asked Carmine.

"She's up on a shelf with her reattached tail where Spicey can't see her. We need to go," she said as she grabbed Butcher Jim's arm.

"How about meeting for breakfast tomorrow at 8:30?"

Patnude answered, "Okay."

"Carmine has changed since Kipfer took over running her 24-hour convenience store. She and Butcher Jim, who would have thought," Jackie stated.

"I know. What are your plans for tomorrow?"

"You mean like a date day?"

"Yes."

"I can do breakfast, but then I have several appointments during the day. I'm available for an early dinner and a movie though. However, it's your turn to buy, remember?"

"I do remember."

"Why don't you buy us some wine and we can sit on the lounges on the other side of the pool and chat. I'll go grab a spot."

Patnude watched Jackie as she got up and walked to the other side of the pool. She looked as good from the back as she did from the front. He wondered why she was still available, if she was available. When Patnude returned with their two glasses of wine, two men were talking with Jackie.

"Patnude, this is Bob and Robert, or is it Robert and Bob?" Jackie stated and asked.

"Congratulations on your engagement," Robert said as he shook hands with

Patnude. "When is the wedding?"

"We are still in the planning stage," Jackie answered as she smiled and winked her right eye at Patnude. "We need to schedule it when there are as few deaths as possible in Globe. Don't forget, if you ever need a good mortician to handle a funeral, give Patnude a call. He is one of the best."

"Are you really a mortician?" Bob or Robert asked.

"Yes, I am, with Best Funeral Home in Globe, Arizona."

Bob and Robert left as Patnude handed Jackie her glass of wine.

Jackie smiled as she made a toast, "Here's to our engagement," as she clinked her wine glass three times with Patnude.

"It appears you have no problem meeting new male friends when you are wearing your bathing suit," Patnude observed.

"Thankfully my fiancé showed up in time to save me from Robert and Bob."

"How long have we been engaged?"

"Just a short time, but nevertheless we are engaged. Now tell me how and what you are doing? You haven't called me since I bought you dinner. Why are you here at the Valley Ho? I didn't see your white Impala in the parking lot. Where did you park? How long will you be staying here and what are your plans besides an early dinner and movie with me tomorrow? Well, answer at least one of my questions."

"I'm driving Sissie's orange Mini Cooper S, which I guess is mine now."

"You're driving an orange Mini Cooper? My fiancé is more exciting by the minute. I would never have guessed an orange Mini Cooper. I have no idea what could be next."

"I think the Mini Cooper is it for me right now. I'm still just a boring mortician from Globe."

"How are you doing in regard to Sissie's death?"

"Much better. I've accepted that Sissie has died and is not coming back. I know she'd insist on me getting on with my life, which I think I'm slowly doing. After all, I am driving an orange Mini Cooper and sitting by the pool next to a beautiful woman in a sexy bathing suit, drinking a glass of wine—plus, I'm her newly designated emergency fiancé."

Jackie smiled as she took a sip of her wine and looked at Patnude, "And a much-needed designated fiancé tonight and who knows maybe again tomorrow."

Jackie and Patnude finished their wine, took a quick swim and went to their respective rooms for the night. They both were thinking of one another as they fell asleep in their individual rooms and beds.

A Perfect Get-Out-of-Town Weekend

Jackie and Patnude both showed up at exactly at 8:30 for breakfast. Jackie was no longer in her bathing suit, but instead what appeared to be her standard work uniform.

"Do you recognize me this morning?" asked Jackie.

Patnude looked Jackie over very slowly. "Yes, I do recognize you, it's my favorite fiancée in her work clothes."

Carmine and Butcher Jim showed up wearing shorts and t-shirts. The t-shirts had printed on the front and back in large yellow letters outlined in black, "Butcher Jim's Butcher Shop, Globe, Arizona."

Jackie had already secured their table.

As they were sitting down, Carmine blurted out, "I got a call from my mother that the police had arrested Mrs. Schafer for the murder of Triple S. Can you believe that? Although nobody who knew Triple S believed he would clean a loaded gun."

Butcher Jim added, "Triple S was a safety freak when it came to guns."

Patnude just nodded and was pleased that Mrs. Schafer was arrested. Maybe there is justice after all.

"What are your plans for today and tonight?" Carmine asked.

"I have several business appointments today, and then Patnude and I will have an early dinner and then maybe go to a movie" Jackie stated.

Carmine kicked Butcher Jim under the table and mouthed, "I bet they don't make it to a movie." She then looked back at Patnude and asked, "What about you?"

"I'm going to shop for a new suit and maybe a sport jacket. Maybe go to the art museum."

"Don't do that today," Jackie interjected. "I'd like to tour the art museum, so why don't we do that tomorrow? Maybe Carmine and Butcher Jim could join us."

"We would like that. Let's do the art museum together tomorrow afternoon," Carmine proposed.

After breakfast Patnude walked Jackie to her car. "What time will you be back?"

"Sometime between 2:00 and 3:00, I think. I'll call you when I'm back.

Patnude purchased a new dark gray suit and a light tan blazer, which was the second sport jacket he owned. He thought Sissie would be pleased with him since he was now driving her Mini Cooper, bought a light tan blazer and had a dinner date with Jackie Snow. He also added that he was also Jackie's emergency designated fiancé. He was making progress.

His phone ran, breaking up his thoughts.

"Hi, I've finished my meetings and am back in my room. Come by and pick me up!"

"Okay, see you in five minutes. What's your room number?"

"201."

Patnude knocked on the door of room 201 several times before Jackie answered. She was wearing a black sleeveless dress.

"Sorry, I decided to wear a dress. Will you zip me up in back, please?" Jackie turned around so her back was facing Patnude.

"Very good, Sissie trained you well. Let me slip on my shoes and I'm ready. Are you really wearing a blazer? Is that yours? Let's go."

Jackie grabbed Patnude's hand as she pulled him out of her room and kissed him on the cheek as she whispered in his ear, "My fiancé looks handsome tonight."

"My fiancée, as usual, looks beautiful tonight."

"Handsome and beautiful, we must make quite a couple."

Sunday morning Jackie woke up first and decided to brew some hotel room coffee. Patnude was still sleeping. She thought a late afternoon dinner with a bottle of wine turned into a long pleasant evening of intimacy with Patnude, who woke up as the coffee finished brewing. He looked up and saw Jackie, nude of course, sipping her freshly brewed cup of coffee.

"Would you like some coffee?"

"I'll have a sip of yours after I run to the bathroom."

When Patnude returned, Jackie was waiting for him in bed. After a few sips of coffee by each of them, a mutual decision was made to be intimate again.

Patnude and Jackie met Carmine and Butcher Jim for brunch before going to the Phoenix Art Museum.

"What movie did you see last night?" Carmine asked.

"We couldn't decide on what to see, so we just sat around and chatted for a while," Jackie answered.

Carmine gently kicked Butcher Jim under the table, smiled and mouthed, "I told you so."

After touring the Phoenix Art Museum, Carmine and Butcher Jim returned to Globe. Patnude and Jackie had the rest of the weekend together. They decided to return to the Valley Ho and enjoy each other's company.

Patnude and Jackie were sitting next to each other by the pool and Jackie was wearing her bathing suit. She just walked back bringing a glass of wine for each of them. Of course, Patnude had the pleasure of watching her going and coming.

"After we finish our wine and take a swim, let's go back to my room. I would like to take a nap before we go to dinner," Jackie said.

"Okay," Patnude smilingly responded.

"Patnude, I very much enjoyed being with you last night and would like to continue being with you. However, I think I can understand, or maybe accept, if our relationship moved too fast for you. I don't know how you feel when you lose someone you love very much. I'm not Sissie and do not want to be compared to her if our relationship continues. I would like it to, but don't forget you are driving an orange Mini Cooper now."

"I know you are not Sissie and I will never expect you to be her, nor will I ever compare you to her. I wasn't expecting last night, but I also enjoyed being with you and would like to continue being with you. In fact, let's forget about a swim and take our wine back to my room."

Patnude picked up the two glasses of wine, they got up, and Jackie put her arm around Patnude's waist as they headed to his room at the Valley Ho.

As expected, Patnude and Jackie became a couple after their weekend in Scottsdale. So much so that I.M. and Famine frequently invited them over for Famine's favorite dinner, liver and onions, which Jackie always gleefully accepted and Patnude had no choice but to accept.

However, he still required at least two Manhattans.

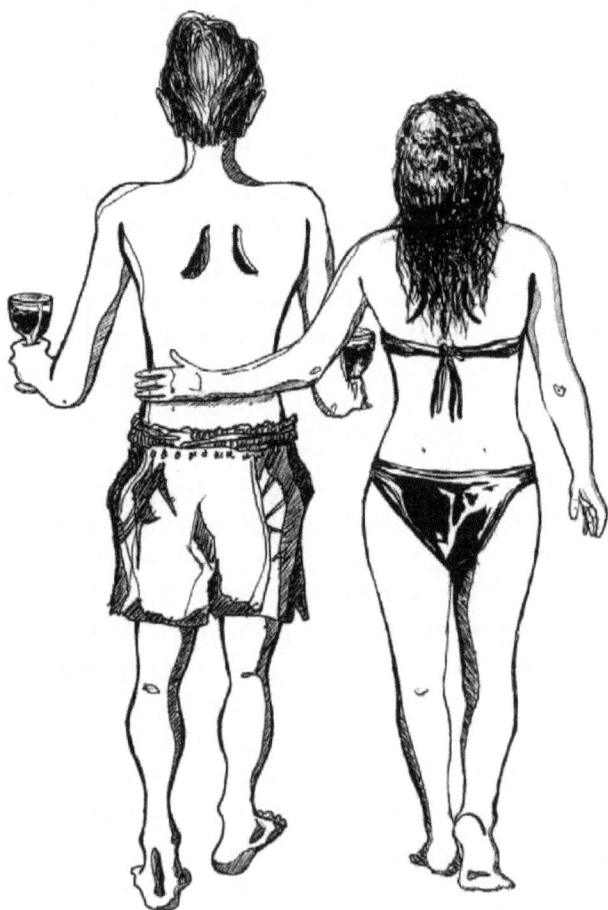

Acknowledgments

I must thank all of the people who helped me with Patnude. My wife Cassandra spent many hours typing, critiquing and making revisions to Patnude. Bree Finnegan and Kellie Teskey for their review and editing along with their kindly comments and suggestions, at least most were kindly, for improving Patnude. And, Peggy Aylett, who presides over a small writing class, here in Phoenix over our winter months, that got me started on "Patnude" with one of her writing assignments. Also, Thomas Rodriguez, who created all of the much appreciated illustrations for "Patnude." And, finally to Nikos Ligidakis, with my publisher Inkwell Books, for his faith and support.

www.ingramcontent.com/pod-product-compliance
Lightning Source LLC
Chambersburg PA
CBHW030926090426
42737CB00007B/338